CREATIVE PARENTHOOD

Advantages You Can Give
Your Child

CREATIVE PARENTHOOD

Advantages You Can Give
Your Child

FRANK CHEAVENS

WORD BOOKS, PUBLISHER, WACO, TEXAS

To a creative family
John and Lynda Cheavens
and their children
Carolyn, John Dwain, Ted, and Emily

Contents

7

Preface

THIS book is written not only with the aim of giving information to parents about the best attitudes and methods of child-rearing, but with the confidence that parents will apply their new knowledge.

In the main, we have discovered that such an application of knowledge comes only after the person becomes emotionally involved with the factual material he learns. Fortunately, one of the best ways of involvement is also a natural, enjoyable thing. This is simply that as you learn something, you discuss it with a friend or acquaintance who perhaps has similar needs to yours. A group of parents in a neighborhood can get together socially and discuss their common problems in child-rearing. Neighbors can do the same thing over the fence.

After you have read this book I hope that you will both share it with friends and neighbors and use it as a basis for discussing your common problems. From such discussions many wonderful things can result. People become better friends and in so doing develop security. The learning from a sound book is reinforced as it is shared and talked about. Parents become better parents and children become better children.

That this book should fulfill this aim is the purpose of the author. I can envision groups of parents in neighborhoods, or from clubs or churches, meeting together periodically to talk over the principles and methods presented. Emerging from this will be friendship, improved communication, and happier families.

Will you personally take upon yourself the getting together of such groups? You will be doing people a great favor, and you will be helping yourself. I wish you well as you do this good thing!

Introduction:
The Background of These Guidelines

WHAT can you do that will help your child develop to his highest potential? The pages that follow are devoted to answering this question. For a number of years, as a professional worker in the field, I have conducted numerous conferences with groups of parents, discussing parent-child relations. Many of these have been P.T.A. meetings. Others have been in churches; still others have been independent child-study groups.

For about two years I worked on a research project having to do with parent-child relations. In this connection we organized group discussions all over the city of Austin, Texas, and extended our services to other nearby cities and towns. The positive results of this project can be found in *Changing Parental Attitudes through Group Discussion.*[1]

In addition to these activities, over a long stretch of time I have taught college courses in child psychology. My best and most eager students have usually been alert young parents, including a sizable number of expectant mothers.

Extensive records have been kept of many of these meetings. These records include the questions of parents, their observations, and the results of their valuable down-to-earth experiences.

The following chapters are a report of one of the best of these series of meetings. It probably comes close to giving a complete coverage of the true essentials of parent-child relations and has special appeal in that so much of the content arises from the group members.

While the personalities comprising the group are real, they have all been given fictitious names for their protection. The report is taken from extensive notes and of course is not verbatim. The fullness of the spontaneous discussions is impossible to recapture on the printed page—the experiences, opinions, immediate feelings, and the general attitudes of the group members to child-rearing. Usually each meeting had one coffee-break. What went on during these breaks—the quips, wisecracks, and the interesting side-talk—was also interesting and important, but unrecorded.

The members of the group are all real people whom I can see quite clearly. The clear memory of the role of each one in group discussion is supplemented by notes and records. Naturally, the report of discussions is edited. A complete record perhaps would have made a volume of formidable length. Here, then, is a cast of the real-life characters comprising our discussion group.

Mr. Inman was a dark-headed, earnest young father of two lively boys. His wife could not attend the discussion but he carried to her the reports of all the meetings.

Mrs. Lovelace was a blonde, an animated young mother of four children, with a keen interest in the workable methods of successful child-rearing, but with just as intense an interest in the reasons underlying these common sense methods.

Mrs. Sonneman was an intellectual type, with light brown hair, a rather long face, not pretty, but with friendly, inquiring, wide gray eyes, a sensitive, beautifully carved mouth. The mother of two children, a boy in the second grade and a five-year-old girl, she had recently completed an M.A. with most of its emphasis on child psychology. She read widely and wanted scientific reasons for everything, if they were available.

Mrs. Putnam had been out of college just a few years. She was one of the three women who were pregnant. Because she could always laugh at herself, she could easily get others to laugh with her. She was short and chubby (actually quite overweight) with twinkling brown eyes and brown hair.

Mrs. Kastly was twenty-five years old, with a sun-freckled sensitive complexion. She was a practical, matter-of-fact person who was a real help to others during emergencies. Also she was pregnant and was to have her second child.

Mr. Shelby, a nice person to be around, had a quick responsive smile that symbolized his outgoing nature. He was friendly and easy to talk with. A former athlete who was beginning to let himself go soft and was putting on more weight than he should, he drank and ate too much and showed guilt about his excesses. But along with all of this he was very tolerant of others. He was the

father of three boys, eight, six, and four years old. His wife could
not attend the sessions.

Mr. Victor, thirty-five years of age, vigorous and strong, had
prematurely graying dark hair. He was very analytical and widely
read, and was highly motivated to be the best father he could be.
Under other circumstances he might have done well in the academic
field. He had, nevertheless, become proficient in his business of
accounting and was in a high bracket financially.

Mrs. Victor was the same age as her husband but looked at
least ten years younger. She was very blonde and very sociable. A
great many of her mornings were spent at bridge or playing golf.
She was also a competent painter and had begun to gain a great
deal of local recognition for the excellence of her work. The Victors
had two boys aged nine and six.

Mrs. Dana, a small woman with a kind face and a soft voice,
was very responsive to others. She had a great capacity for love
and was the mother of six fine boys ranging in age from two to
thirteen.

Mrs. Wallace was thirty years old and a real morale builder in
the group. She spent much of her spare time gardening which gave
her a perennial tan. She had startlingly blue eyes, dark hair, and
a very trim figure of medium height. She had two children, an
eight-year-old girl, and a five-year-old boy. Devoutly religious and
loyal to her church, she was not at all dogmatic but was constantly
showing thoughtfulness of others and consideration for their points
of view. She was the third pregnant woman in the group.

Mr. Wallace was also the outdoor type, lean, strong and re-
sourceful. Like his wife, he had a deep, year-round tan. He spent
much of his spare time hunting, fishing, and water-skiing.

Mrs. Zimmer was the only representative in the group of a
broken family. Apparently her former husband, from whom she
was divorced, was a philandering ne'er-do-well. She worked as a
secretary and was fortunate in having her very fine and vigorous
mother to take care of the home and to be a companion to the
children, two girls of seven and three. Apparently all four had
harmonious relations. Mrs. Zimmer, a personable woman of thirty,
had glossy brown hair, large brown eyes and a nice figure. She
had perhaps an excess of anxiety about her role as a mother and a
provider, and about the absence of a father-figure for the girls.
Although she had many male admirers (some of them ineligible
for marriage) and was in favor of remarriage, she had at that time
not found the right person.

These twelve made up the discussion group. Four more had
started but dropped out after the first few meetings. The remaining twelve were eager to come and were present except in unavoidable circumstances.

Without exception they all felt that they became better parents
as the result of the discussions. Probably this resulted from an increased understanding of all their problems and their solutions. In
a few instances the leader had extended conferences with members
which also seemed to result in a lowering of tensions, perhaps because of the catharsis of talking about stressful situations.

The objective study in Austin, mentioned above, demonstrated
clearly not only that our spontaneous group discussions in series
helped members become better parents but also, somewhat to my
surprise, that the children also improved, quite evidently as a result of parental improvement. My feeling had been that any improvement in the children would take place long after each series
of discussions closed rather than in the brief time which elapsed between our measurements.

I came out of this experience with a deep conviction that discussions of the kind we had in Austin should be organized in all
areas all over the country. Such discussions could undoubtedly go
far toward the amelioration of our serious social problems today.

In addition to the professional book reporting our work in detail, written by Dr. Carl Hereford, clinical psychologist, I wrote a
booklet for discussion leaders which has been and is being widely
used in a variety of locations.[2] It was published on a nonprofit basis
and is available at the Hogg Foundation for Mental Health at the
University of Texas, Austin, or at the materials center of the National Institute for Mental Health in New York.

The objective of the present book is to present general principles
that are applicable in many specific cases, in the hope that each
reader will find the clues to meet his own. Specific methods and
techniques are presented here, of course, but it is the attitudes that
provide and accompany them that loom most important.

You wish to give your children great advantages. Most of these
advantages are intangibles that result from constructive attitudes.
Attitudes produce behavior, and constructive attitudes result in
constructive behavior. Fortunately, you can give your children
most of these great advantages through the development of desirable attitudes and desirable behavior.

It hardly needs emphasizing that good parents, in every sense
of the word, make for good families. It is our hope that as the result of the following pages there will be improved parents and im-

proved families. You can be a creative parent, and you can give your children the most important advantages of all by helping them develop constructive, creative attitudes and behavior.

Maturation and growth are slow and long drawn out; they cannot be forced. Be patient with your children. Enjoy them, and they will enjoy you. Give them time to mature and the right kind of atmosphere in which to do it. Your reward will be the pleasure of watching them achieve their highest potential of development.

FOOTNOTES

1. Carl F. Hereford. *Changing Parental Attitudes through Group Discussion.* (Austin, Texas: The Hogg Foundation for Mental Health. The University of Texas, 1963).

2. Frank Cheavens. *Leading Group Discussions.* (Austin, Texas: The Hogg Foundation for Mental Health, 1958).

1. You Can Help Your Child *

THE MAJOR purpose of these discussions is to help you know what you can do that will result in the best development of your child. Every child has certain wonderful potentials. Most children do not develop those to their fullest. Most human beings do not even come close to their maximum in any area of life. What are the things you can do, the situations you can provide, that will help your child come close to realizing his potential?

Each person has a potential in socially satisfying relationships, in mental development, and in achievement generally—including creativity. Physical well-being contributes to each of these. Are there those things you can provide or do that will mean that your child has the best chance of development in each of these areas? Is there a social climate you can establish in the home that will provide the foundation for the most satisfying social relationships? Is there a mental environment you can create which will mean that your child's mind will develop to its fullest? Is there something you can do to foster healthy physical growth that will contribute to both mental and social growth?

The answer to each of these questions in general is yes. We know that there are influences other than yours as parents that affect your child's welfare. No parent is all-powerful. But we are interested here in your parental attitudes and behavior that have significant outcomes for your children. In my many contacts I have found that most parents want to do the best job they can in rearing

* This was a brief introductory talk to the discussions by the leader.

their children. If they do not do a good job it is usually because they do not know how.

Knowing how to help your children is not a matter of simple mechanics. If something goes wrong with your sewing machine or your car, there is a specific remedy for the trouble. A metal part is worn out or broken, or something needs adjusting. The mechanic for either machine has a definite remedy for the trouble.

In helping your children no one can give you neat, exact directions. Human development is too complex, too much an individual matter, for mechanical prescriptions. Human relations, as between parents and children, have too many delicate and intangible nuances for a series of discussions of this kind to hand out recipes, cookbook fashion, which all of you can apply to all of your children.

But the good news is that we do know certain broad principles whose application brings good results. We have accumulated a great deal of evidence to help us know this. These principles and their use we give you in this series.

Specifics are often helpful. There are some particular problems relating to children about which we have a wealth of knowledge. Where it is possible to present guidelines on specific problems which might be the problems of your children, we shall try to do it. At least two discussions, perhaps even more, will be devoted to such specific problems and what is known about their solution. In other discussions, specific problems will be dealt with where applicable, along with the broader, general principles.

Today's parents are interested not so much in opinions as in established facts. Much of the material I shall present here is based upon accumulated knowledge which comes largely from scientifically designed investigation. Some of these investigations are so fascinating that I shall talk about them rather fully. Some of them are exploratory and it is too early to know their exact meaning. In certain cases we have conflicting evidence. In each instance we shall try to indicate the nature and the extent of the evidence. It is the evidence that you are interested in.

What a pleasant task it is to be able to give parents an optimistic message about their children's development! There was a time when parents felt that some intangible fate had determined ahead of time what the child would turn out to be, and they themselves could do nothing to alter it. Now we know that, in the main, most of the factors determining a child's development are controllable. There are definite causes for behavior and attitudes. In the early and most important years the parents create most of the child's environment. This means that parents can do a great deal for the child to help him achieve his optimal development, satisfactions, and happiness.

Parental attitudes are the key. Attitudes are subject to our control. We can improve our attitudes. We have no negative attitude that cannot be changed to a positive one.

2. The Important Beginning

DR. CHEAVENS: As you may imagine, the list of topics for discussion in this all-important area of child-parent relationships includes all the mother can do during pregnancy to further the welfare of the unborn infant. So this is the point from which we initiate our discussions.

Most of us would assume that the pregnant woman would obviously be under the care of a good doctor, yet it is astounding how many women in the United States have no medical care during pregnancy.

MRS. KASTLY: I had no idea that any pregnant woman in our country went without medical care. Do you know how many?

DR. CHEAVENS: The figures I have come from the 1963 Kennedy report. In 138 large cities 455,000 women went without medical care, not only during pregnancy, but also following the birth of the baby.[1] (The group showed consternation over these figures in a brief discussion of the problem, and two members volunteered to check locally about medical facilities for pregnant women in poverty.)

DR. CHEAVENS: From the time of conception there is a great deal the pregnant woman can do to make sure the unborn baby is getting his best start.

We are all concerned about product quality. Manufacturing concerns employ expert researchers to see that every factor is taken care of to guarantee production of the most useful and durable articles. In agriculture we go to no end of trouble to improve livestock and crops. Today's far-seeing parent has the same attitude. He is eager to do all within his power to make sure that his child will be the best possible human product. And this kind of parent knows the importance of the fetal period in this process.

In most cities of any size there are classes of instruction for parents during this period before the baby is born. More will be said later about a special type of training which may be available in your community. Perhaps as we realize more and more the importance of education, we shall establish classes of instruction on a nationwide scale available to all prospective parents. We have had this nationwide vision concerning livestock and crops but thus far not for parents. This indicates a strange distortion of values.

Parents' Feelings About the Expected Infant

Recently I talked with a young couple who had just discovered that a baby was on its way. This was an unplanned event and something of a surprise. Even so, this couple was very happy about the prospect.

Their pleasure will actually benefit the unborn child. The babies of mothers who willingly accept the pregnancy and are happy about it are usually happier, healthier babies than those whose mothers are unhappy about it. I see we have a question.

MRS. SHELBY: Do we have any scientific basis for what you are saying?

DR. CHEAVENS: Yes. A study made in San Francisco found there was a close relationship between mothers' unhappiness about pregnancy and their babies who were described as "upset."[72] Unhappy mothers had more babies who seemed disturbed.

Even mothers who look forward to having the baby will have periods of mixed emotions. Women with the best attitudes may at times feel rebellious. There might be a good many reasons for this. A person sometimes just has a bad day, or is not feeling well physically. Besides, another child brings added responsibilities and added expense.

MRS. PUTNAM: When you're sick to death every morning, it's a bit hard to be happy about pregnancy. (Laughter) Go on and laugh. It's not a laughing matter to me. (More laughter, and Mrs. Putnam joins in.)

MRS. SHELBY: Part of morning sickness may be due to fear or too much tension. Part of it is psychological.

MRS. PUTNAM: I wish I could believe that.

MR. SHELBY: The husband of the pregnant woman sometimes has morning sickness. I'm a prime example. I was just as sick as my wife. Was mine physical or psychological? (Laughter from the group)

Dr. CHEAVENS: I think there's something in what Mrs. Shelby is saying. There are recorded cases of women whose morning sickness was greatly reduced by reducing tension and fear.

Some mothers are extremely rebellious about the thought of the coming baby. Nearly all who have such an attitude, or even those who merely have passing periods of rebellion, usually also have considerable guilt about their negative attitudes. Many women find the thought of carrying the baby nine months and all the added burdens that will come later very distasteful. But they also would like to change their attitude about it.

Mrs. KASTLY: Is there anything a woman can do about it if she's rebellious about being pregnant?

Dr. CHEAVENS: Yes, there is. First she can be honest with herself about all her feelings, bringing them out into the open where they can be examined clearly. She can talk about them with somebody who understands, someone who will accept her negative emotions and not lecture or scold her about them but just try to get her point of view. Usually the doctor is such a person. Some tolerant friend might do. Talking about the rejection of childbearing, or the passing feelings of unpleasantness about it, nearly always helps to cut down on those unwelcome thoughts and feelings. Sharing the burden somehow tends to lighten it.

It also helps to find out *why* she is rejecting pregnancy, or why there are days when her condition is unwelcome. Usually fear lies behind the negative attitude. She may be afraid she will lose her nice figure or that she is not going to have as much freedom as before. She may dread the experience of childbirth. Later, we shall talk much more fully about this last fear. Anyway, knowing what the fear is will help the person to cope with it. Doing something about fears nearly always helps do away with them. And nearly always if the woman gets rid of her fear, she will also get rid of her generally unpleasant feelings about being pregnant.

The husband's reactions to his wife's carrying their child are a factor in fetal development because his wife is affected by him. His pleasure usually increases hers. His optimism and confidence are contagious. And his wife would usually need great inner strength not to be influenced by his negative reactions.

Mrs. WALLACE: I think my religious faith helped to smooth out my bad days during pregnancy more than anything else.

Mrs. DANA: I can say the same thing, and I've been through it six times.

MRS. PUTNAM: I'm not doubting your word, but just how did it help?

MRS. WALLACE: I find that I always feel better after I pray about things. It relieves my worry and makes me feel things are going to come out all right. I face things more optimistically.

MRS. DANA: My religion is comforting and reassuring. It gives me confidence instead of fear. And love is the heart of religion, and an attitude of love solves most problems.

MRS. PUTNAM: Both of you seem to have a practical, positive religion, and I can see that it might help.

The Broader Picture of Parental Emotions

DR. CHEAVENS: What has just been said about the husband's attitude should be kept in mind in the following discussion, even though most of it will be addressed to the wife. First a word of reassurance—it can be expected that most people in any one day will go through a variety of emotions including happiness, sadness, fear, and anger. There are no indications that these everyday passing emotions of the mother have any bad effects upon the unborn infant. There is no evidence, either, that even a serious short emotional upset will affect the fetus adversely, although our knowledge here is far from being complete. More research is needed in this area. A commonsense approach would be for the mother to avoid serious emotional disturbances as much as possible.

Most of the facts we possess have to do with long-drawn-out disturbances. A long-lasting upsetting emotion affects the hormonal balances of the mother, and her hormonal imbalances affect the unborn child. Anxiety, sadness, or anger over long periods of time have harmful effects upon the fetus. Dr. Lester W. Sontag of the Fels Institute found that an emotional disturbance of the mother causes stimulated activity in the fetus.[3] This is true for both short and long periods of time. Over a long period of time the fetus might have too much stimulated activity.

It is of interest that animal experiments show similar results. Experimenters caused anxiety in pregnant rats and studied the effects of this anxiety on the babies. The effects were observed not only 30 to 40 days after birth, but much later—130 days to 140 days after birth.[4] The babies were much more emotional than those of mother rats that hadn't been made anxious, and they kept on being more emotional. Of course, we have to be careful in drawing conclusions about human beings from experiments with animals. But here they give us some added evidence.

We are to have two reports from members, and perhaps we should hear them now. Mrs. Sonneman will give hers first, and she will be followed by Mrs. Kastly.

Relationship of Child and Mother

MRS. SONNEMAN: Some of us have been reading about an investigation that was carried out in Uganda.[5] These African infants (308 of them) were found to be very advanced in comparison with the average Western infant. The Uganda infant is able to hold its head erect around nine hours after birth as compared with six weeks for Western infants. The two-day-old Uganda child can hold head erect and back straight and focus eyes on the examiner (eight weeks for Western children). Assuming a sitting position is possible for the Uganda child at seven weeks (twenty weeks for Western children). The Uganda child walks to a Gesell box—a gadget designed for studying the behavior of infants—and looks inside at seven months (fifteen months for Western children). Likewise in speech development (which of all early abilities is most closely linked with later intelligence), in social development, in general adaptability to many situations, the Uganda child is far ahead.

The question that comes to my mind is why this fast development takes place. There seems to be no certain answer. The best we can do is to set out some of the probabilities, as suggested by the author.

First, the Uganda mother, when she knows she has conceived, makes the welfare of the unborn child her major concern. Traditionally the Ugandas believe that the mother's unhappy thoughts are not good for the unborn child and that happy thoughts will make for a better child. The mother keeps herself happy, and others help with this. Everybody tries to avoid emotional disturbances. This ties in with our discussion about the emotions.

Following birth, the child and the mother are in constant contact with each other day and night. Feeding is by demand. There is much cuddling, caressing and soft speech. The mother aids and encourages the child in simple learning. This sort of thing will help any baby be happier.

Of course, you are probably thinking that many mothers in many

countries have happy pregnancies and give their infants ample
affection. Yet their babies are not as advanced as these in Uganda.
We just do not know all the causes of the fast development of the
Uganda babies. The authors made a number of suggestions. There
may be factors of diet, and Dr. Geber says they are magnificently
fed. The great vitality of the mothers, or heredity, or a combination
of a number of causes like these might be responsible.

For most of the Uganda children this fast development seems to
stop at about the third year. This may be because weaning at this
time is abrupt and harsh. Having experienced a close relationship
with his mother, the young child is suddenly pushed away; sometimes he is even sent to live with a relative who is almost a stranger
to him. In the light of what we know about the damage to child
personality of such separations, and of rejection, we could predict
that this would set the child back. Since the beginnings of the
Uganda infant are so good, it's too bad the process is interrupted.
Maybe, as the study of the Uganda babies continues, facts may be
uncovered that will help babies everywhere.

MRS. KASTLY: My report has a bearing here. It comes from an
investigator who tried to find out the connection between the personality of twenty mothers and their colicky babies who cried too
much. He compared these mothers with twenty mothers of babies
who did not have much colic and did not cry very much.[6] Some of
the differences between the two groups of mothers were easy to
pick out. The mothers of the colicky babies had been more upset
all during pregnancy and after. They were sad after the baby's
birth and were very tense, particularly when the baby cried. They
had trouble knowing what the baby's crying was all about. Handling the baby made them nervous. These mothers described themselves as habitually tense and nervous.

In contrast, the mothers of the noncolicky, happier babies were
more relaxed during pregnancy and in their relations with the infant after birth. It seems that emotions such as grief, hostility or
anger, anxiety, or fear that just go on and on are not good for the
unborn baby. When you begin to think about how many expectant
mothers go through long periods of being emotionally upset, you
know that a great many babies are the worse for it.

DR. CHEAVENS: It's easy to see that a mother who finds herself
caught in a long-drawn-out emotional disturbance should try to do
everything possible to make her frame of mind better. Discussing
problems with somebody one can trust is often enough to break the
pattern. If this does not work, a mother should go to a good psychi-
atrist or a psychologist.

The methods that will help to break up a pattern of disturbing emotions follow about the same line as the suggestions made above about getting rid of poor attitudes toward pregnancy. Talk about the disturbance to some understanding person. Bring it all out in the open and examine it. Try to find the cause and do something about it.

FOOTNOTES

1. J. F. Kennedy, "Message from the President of the U.S. relative to mental illness and mental retardation," *American Psychologist* 18 (1963), 280–89.

2. Ashley Montagu, *Life Before Birth* (New York: New American Library, Signet Books, 1965), p. 165.

3. Ibid., pp. 163–64.

4. W. R. Thompson, "Influence of Prenatal Anxiety on Emotionality in Young Rats," *Science* 125:698–99.

5. Marcelle Geber, "The Psychomotor Development of African Children in the First Year, and the Influences of Maternal Behavior," *Journal of Social Psychology* 47 (1958), 185–195.

6. Martin Lakin, *Personality Factors in Mothers of Excessively Crying (colicky) Infants*, Monograph of the Society for Research in Child Development (Yellow Springs, Ohio: The Antioch Press), series 64, vol. 22 (1957), 19–30.

3. Advantages You Can Give Your Child During Pregnancy

DR. CHEAVENS: I have been asked by several members of the group to give a brief discussion of what is called natural childbirth. What I have to say will be supplemented by reports gathered by three of our members, all of whom have access to large libraries, one of which is in our local medical school.

Childbirth without Fear

For a number of years investigators have known that the tensions caused by fear made pain more intense and harder to bear. Freedom from fear reduces tension and this in turn reduces pain.

Over twenty years ago some obstetricians had enough insight to see that pregnancy itself and the fear of childbirth were the cause of a great deal of worry. These persisting fears in turn made the entire period of gestation one of many trying problems. Worry made morning sickness worse and the women generally more uncomfortable. These obstetricians reasoned that anxiety and fear made the pain of childbirth either worse or harder to endure. We know that tension generally makes pain worse. This is true in the dentist's chair, or with pain from any cause. Relieving the anxiety during the prenatal period, then, would be an all-round help to the mother, and when labor came, she would probably have less pain, or at least would be able to bear the pain better.

One of the pioneers in this field, whose contributions have been immensely valuable, was the English obstetrician Dr. Grantly Dick-Read. His books on childbirth have been read by a great many people, and his book *Childbirth without Fear* [1] has been translated into eleven languages and has had a great influence on obstetrical practices all over the world. (It is now available as a paperback.[2]) The theme of the book is that most of the mother's suffering in childbirth is caused by tension due to fear, and that if the fear can be taken away, tension will be reduced and that will mean less discomfort during both gestation and childbirth. This fear-tension process is usually changed by Dr. Dick-Read's method, and there are good results from what the mother both learns and does. She is given all kinds of helpful information about the prenatal period and about childbirth.

The more the expectant mother learns, the more her fears are reduced and the less tension she has. She begins to be more comfortable. The acquisition of this useful knowledge in itself is tension-reducing. The joys and satisfactions of having a child are talked about a great deal in the training course. The instruction is done ideally in groups, but sometimes a physician or a nurse may give individual instruction. Some women take the training by studying the book alone.

There is a great deal to the training course as one may see from reading the book. The woman is given a set of good exercises to strengthen her muscles. She is instructed in stimulating breathing exercises that help her feel better. She is also taught how to relax by the Edmund Jacobson method. This method of relaxation is something everyone in our hurrying world ought to learn, anyway. The mother is given guidance about the kind of diet that is best. There are helpful instructions for husbands, too, whose part during the prenatal period and childbirth is very important, as has already been indicated.[3]

The result of this educational process is that a majority of the mothers are reported to find childbirth an enriching experience, rather than one of dreadful pain.[4] Many report real satisfaction during the period of labor. However, I think it would be a mistake for anyone to take the Dick-Read method of training with the idea of having a "painless" childbirth without any anesthetics or analgesics. If one takes the recommended training with the idea of getting in as good physical condition as possible for her own sake and for the sake of the baby, the training will do good and there will be no disappointment.[5] It is possible one will get by with less discomfort and less help from anesthetics or analgesics. The obstetricians who advocate the natural childbirth training do not withhold the necessary help the mother may need from drugs or from the usual surgery.

There has been considerable debate in the United States over
the question of natural childbirth. Part of the trouble arose because
of extremists on both sides. Whenever one finds much emotion entering into the discussion of an issue like this, it becomes hard to
find the facts.

The opponents of natural childbirth became bitter and irrational
in fighting it. Some of the fanatics on the side of natural childbirth
overemphasized the goal of painlessness, and a few are reported
to have insisted that the woman in labor should refuse all analgesics
and anesthetics. The way it stands now, both of these extremes are
rejected by most obstetricians. The obstetricians who are for natural childbirth recommend any of the available scientific helps when
they are needed. Among the natural childbirth advocates are the
recognized authorities on obstetrics at the Yale University Medical
School, such as Dr. Milton J. Senn and Dr. C. Lee Buxton, whose
articles and books on the topic are widely read.[6]

The first of our reports will be given by Mrs. Lovelace, who has
dug out some interesting facts.

MRS. LOVELACE: I hope I'm not one of the fanatics Dr. Cheavens mentioned. But I'll have to admit that I am prejudiced in favor
of natural childbirth training, for a very good reason. My first
child was delivered in the conventional way, without benefit of
training. I was afraid and tense and experienced a lot of pain. My
three other children were all born after I had received the natural
childbirth training.

I had so little discomfort and fear with these last three that I am
completely sold on natural childbirth. The experience of giving
birth to these three children was truly a happy one. I have very
little memory of the birth of the first at all, except for the considerable pain I felt.

Results of Natural Childbirth Training

A good many facts have been gathered on this subject. A number
of studies have been carried out in England, using large groups of
mothers who took natural-childbirth training as compared with
mothers who had no training. Dr. Helen Rodway, consultant obstetrician for a large maternity hospital in London, gives the essence
of these studies in an article in the *Journal of Obstetrics and Gynecology*.[7] Most of the studies show the advantage of training or instruction. Dr. Rodway took three groups for comparison. The first
was composed of 1000 women who took the training; the second

was 700 women who attended lectures and talks giving much necessary information about pregnancy and childbirth; the third were 1000 women who took no training and went to no lectures. Dr. Rodway concluded: "the results suggest that education of the expectant mother may be a helpful contributing factor in reducing the incidence of prematurity and perinatal mortality." Among the 700 women who only attended lectures and talks, but did not take the training, it seemed that quite a few on their own went through the complete natural childbirth training schedule. The babies of both the training group and the instructed group had a better chance than the babies whose mothers had no specific education during pregnancy.

Mr. Victor: Dr. Rodway's research didn't establish that the natural childbirth training was superior to the lectures and talks, did it?

Mrs. Lovelace: No, it didn't. Except that it seemed that quite a few of these women under the informative lectures were also taking the natural childbirth training on their own.

Dr. Cheavens: Next, we'll hear from Mrs. Dana.

Mrs. Dana: I'm one who didn't ever have natural childbirth training. The same obstetrician delivered all six of my boys and he's very skillful. I wasn't really fearful about labor, anyway, and my doctor was very conservative in the use of anesthetics. I really never had a bad time with any of the babies. But, I'm really interested in natural childbirth, since most of it is common sense.

The first article I'm reporting on was in the *Ladies Home Journal*.[8] Some of you may have read the article which stated that the medical information gathered over a period of twenty years has been favorable to the natural childbirth training. In this same article Dr. M. E. Davis, professor of obstetrics and gynecology at the University of Chicago, said that training shortened the time of labor, resulted in fewer complications, and reduced the need for analgesics and anesthetics. The same article carried a statement from Dr. Leonard Kimmel, of the Margaret Hague Maternity Hospital of Jersey City, New Jersey, that in his approximately 1000 deliveries by natural childbirth following a training program, his "morbidity rate" for both mother and child compared favorably with the "best hospital rate." He had a record of no deaths of mothers. His "incidence of operative repairs required or done for any injury to the perineum or to the ligaments of the uterus has been zero." When he had formerly done "routine obstetrics on unprepared mothers" there had been many such operations.

The second article was in *Time* telling about five years of natural childbirth practices at St. Mary's hospital in St. Louis, where 1,182 babies had been delivered by these methods. One of the most significant statements made was that "the most die-hard anti-naturalists among obstetricians now recognize the value of prenatal education and exercise." [9]

DR. CHEAVENS: Any discussion?

MRS. VICTOR: It's very hard to find an obstetrician in this area who believes in natural childbirth, isn't it?

MRS. LOVELACE: Yes, that's true, but there are a few available who are very fine obstetricians. Also there is a sister in one of the hospitals who conducts the training classes regularly. The exercises are very relaxing and make you feel wonderful. The aim is to get the pregnant woman in the very best physical and mental condition possible.

MRS: VICTOR: I may not be very progressive, but I think I would rather just get a good obstetrician and turn it all over to him.

MRS. DANA: One good result of all the material on natural childbirth has been to reduce the amounts of anesthetics and analgesics used. All the obstetricians have been influenced to a certain extent. Mine wanted me to exercise, especially to walk, during every pregnancy. He was insistent on a good diet. And, as I said, he was very conservative in using anesthetics.

DR. CHEAVENS: We have a last report to be made by Mrs. Kastly.

MRS. KASTLY: My reading convinced me that the natural childbirth approach was best. My doctor is not against it and told me he would be pleased if I took the training. The birth of my first was rather a bad experience and I hope this second one will be better.

All of my information came from a book in the library written by Dr. H. B. Atlee, head of the Department of Obstetrics and Gynecology of Dalhousie University in Halifax, Nova Scotia. This doctor writes that he regrets the fact that natural childbirth methods have been "touted" as "painless" childbirth, when the methods are really "to make the pain of labor more bearable." [10]

The hospital in which Dr. Atlee practiced had reported twelve hundred cases of delivery by natural childbirth. Of these, 46 percent had spontaneous labor with no sedative and said they would want to repeat the training schedule again. Another 11 percent had spontaneous delivery with only one sedative, and said they would want to take the training again. There were 18 percent who needed "some anesthetic" and "one or two sedatives" but who had spontaneous labor and would willingly repeat the training. Still another 18 percent felt they had been helped by training and would repeat it but had taken one or more sedatives and either a general or spinal anesthetic, with forceps deliveries. Only 7 percent felt the natural childbirth training had not helped and would not repeat the training.

There were some other convincing facts. Dr. Atlee said that in their hospital, prior to the natural childbirth training, resuscitation of newborn infants was a common problem, and "we were constantly suffering anxiety over babies that would not respond because they seemed doped. This anxiety has greatly disappeared among those of us who use the method and it is very gratifying to have baby after baby cry immediately and lustily."

These investigators had kept records on the average time before breathing began with babies whose mothers had taken the natural childbirth training as compared to those whose mothers had not had the training. The time for the infants whose mothers had taken training was from 5 to 10 seconds as compared with more than 20 seconds for the nontraining infants. The time before crying for infants whose mothers had taken the training was 10 to 15 seconds, with an average of 50 seconds required for the infants of the notraining mother. Only 3 percent of the training infants required resuscitation, compared to 15 percent of the nontraining infants.

Observation in the nursery showed training infants' behavior which was "less than good" at only 9 percent, and the nontraining infants at 13 percent. Of the training infants 8 percent were irritable compared to 14 percent of the nontraining infants. Poor relaxation was observed in 7 percent of the training infants and 11 percent of the nontraining group.

This is all very convincing to me, and I don't see why we can't have more doctors using these methods. I'm not expecting miracles, but I think my second experience is going to be better than the first.

Dr. CHEAVENS: The major mistake women make who take the training is to expect no pain during a spontaneous delivery. If a woman enters into the program to get her body in the very best condition possible for the good of her baby, she will profit by it. Naturally, she will turn over all decisions during labor to her obstetrician.

FOOTNOTES

1. Grantly Dick-Read, *Childbirth without Fear*, 2nd ed. (New York: Harper & Row, 1959).
2. Published by Harper & Row.
3. Ibid., pp. 144, 166, 173–86.
4. Ibid., p. 187.
5. Ibid., pp. 187–237.
6. See for instance C. Lee Buxton, *Study of Psychophysical Methods for Relief of Childbirth Pain* (Philadelphia: W. B. Saunders, 1962); Milton J. Senn, "Storm over Childbirth," *McCall's* 90 (February 1963), 40ff.
7. Helen Rodway, "Education for Childbirth and Its Result," *Journal of Obstetrics and Gynecology* 64 (1957), 545–60.
8. "Natural Childbirth, Facts and Fallacies," *Ladies Home Journal* 79 (October 1962), 53ff.
9. *Time*, September 25, 1964, p. 81.
10. H. B. Atlee, *Natural Childbirth* (Springfield, Illinois: Charles C Thomas, 1956), p. 67. The statistics that follow are taken from pp. 62–65.

4. Advantages from Scientific Studies

DR. CHEAVENS: I have become increasingly aware of the interest of today's parents in the contributions science is making to the entire process of child-rearing. In our discussions I have learned that this is what all of you are really seeking.

It is most reassuring to have some facts, to be able to say, "This is well established. This is a guideline that has been verified. I can hold to this with confidence." Our group is perhaps representative of a new approach to life in our generation, in which we no longer trust mere opinion, or the voice of officialdom just because it represents traditional authority. We want to know what is really true. So we shall examine a few of the contributions scientific method is making to the welfare of both child and mother.

That we need more research is obvious. Reliable knowledge pays big dividends in many ways. One of them is to add to the confidence of the physician. This confidence is contagious and is passed on to the patient. As the patient's morale is improved, his chances of good health are improved. So one of the by-products of research is to add to the emotional well-being of the mother and child.

Research is constantly making specific material contributions, such as the new test for phenylketonuria (PKU). This is a rare metabolic disorder in which the infant's body can't take care of certain amino acids, which, becoming toxic, may even affect the brain. Research has shown not only how to detect quickly this infrequent disorder, but also how to counteract its toxic effects.

In the same way, research has shown what to do about the much-publicized Rh-positive–Rh-negative incompatibility, and other similar problems. Much more is now known also about counteracting the effects of high blood pressure (hypertension) and diabetes in the pregnant woman. It is comforting to the expectant mother to realize that science is discovering how to deal more successfully with nearly all these hazards, however infrequently they may occur.

Cigarette Smoking and the Fetus

Many women are not acquainted with the new research about the relationship of the mother's cigarette smoking and the development of the embryo. For a long time it has been known that smoking a cigarette would increase the heartbeat of the fetus, but only recently has it been established that the mother's smoking even half a pack a day is bad for the unborn child.

Over 12,000 women were part of three big studies on the effects of cigarette smoking upon the unborn child. These studies agree that the mother's cigarette smoking reduces the baby's chances of good health.[1] The most recent investigation was made by a team at Johns Hopkins University. Dr. Todd M. Frazier was the director of the project. The information given below came from his report of the project to the American Academy for Cerebral Palsy.

The investigators used as subjects 2,736 pregnant women in Baltimore. They were divided into two equal groups—smokers and nonsmokers. The babies of smoking mothers averaged six ounces lighter at birth, which perhaps shows that the fetus's supply or assimilation of food was not as good as it would have been if the mother hadn't been a smoker. Frazier also reported a 40 to 60 percent larger number of premature births among smoking mothers.

What we don't know is just what it is about smoking cigarettes that causes these troubles. Of course, smoking is bad for the circulation and this would be harmful to the mother's health generally. The smoker also inhales a certain amount of carbon monoxide, which is bad for both mother and fetus.

At first when all the alarming reports were coming in about cigarette smoking and cancer, my personal hope was that a harmless substitute for tobacco could be found. I was forgetting to take into account the carbon monoxide which the smoker inhales, no matter what substance is smoked. Maybe someone will think up a way to get around this, but right now no one has come up with anything of promise.

MRS. PUTNAM (sighing): This comes as a low blow. My doctor told me it was desirable to quit cigarettes. Now I feel I've got to! And it's really my only vice and such an enjoyable one! (Much laughter from the group.) And then there's my weight problem, which will be worse when I quit smoking. Oh, dear me!

MR. SHELBY: I wish that was my only vice. I have a question here. Don't the studies just say the *probability* is greater of having a prematurely born infant?

DR. CHEAVENS: That is a good point. Many women who have smoked during pregnancy have experienced no difficulty and have even had large babies that were physically thriving. The studies merely mean that the chances of having a prematurely born baby are greater for cigarette smokers.

MR. INMAN: But how would a mother feel if she continued smoking, knowing about the chances, and her baby was premature? It seems to me to continue smoking in the face of the evidence is inviting trouble.

A lively discussion of the subject followed, with most of the group expressing the opinion that for the pregnant woman to continue smoking cigarettes was too risky. There were two dissenting opinions.

DR. CHEAVENS: The oxygen supply from the mother to the unborn babe is of great importance. One specific point is that if the fetal brain is to develop as it should, plenty of oxygen must be in the mother's blood. This must be one of several reasons why the breathing exercises suggested in Dr. Dick-Read's and other prenatal training courses are helpful. In line with this is a report that Mrs. Zimmer has volunteered to give from some of her reading.

The Birth Suit

MRS. ZIMMER: Many women have read about the experiments of Dr. O. S. Heyns, head of the Department of Gynecology and Obstetrics, taking place at the University of Witwatersrand, South Africa.[2] He has invented a "birth suit" for the pregnant woman. The investigators have reported that 90 percent of the women who have used it have had greatly reduced pain during labor or no pain at all. This birth suit had been under trial for over ten years at the time of the report. It has made the time of labor shorter and it has cut down on hemorrhaging, and on possible brain-damage to the newborn infant.

It is an "abdominal decompression chamber" made from plastic and covering the mother from chest to feet. The mother can regulate the pressure, reducing it when various muscle tensions occur. This is helpful not only during labor, but to relieve uterus contractions that seem to be frequent during the last months of pregnancy. These contractions are thought by Dr. Heyns and others to cut down on the blood supply to the fetus which in turn reduces the amount of oxygen. It is Dr. Heyns' theory that even these short periods of less oxygen may, and I quote, "affect the degree of intelligence of the child by impairing, however slightly, the development of the brain to its full potential."

The birth suit helps insure the oxygen supply in the baby's blood. One of the aims of this research is to see if the intelligence of these babies who have plenty of oxygen all the time will be higher than that of babies born without benefit of the birth suit. The article also says that this decompression method takes away most of the mother's fears. And usually, as we have said before, less fear means less pain.

Here I have a recent article from the newspaper reporting an interview with a Houston, Texas, obstetrician, Dr. Lawrence E. Lundgren, who exhibited a modified version of the birth suit which is fitted over the mother's abdomen. When she feels a contraction she pushes a button producing a partial vacuum which lifts the abdominal wall and reduces the strength of the contraction. The doctor reports that this device has been used in more than 15,000 deliveries, with absolute safety, shortening the period of labor and reducing pain.

While I have no immediate plans for using the birth suit (laughter from the group), it sounds wonderful. My opinion would be that the use of the birth suit would certainly not do away with the need for the pregnant woman to keep herself in the best possible physical condition by exercise, diet, and peace of mind.

DR. CHEAVENS: Any questions or discussion?

MRS. WALLACE: Do you have any figures about the average time for delivery using the birth suit?

MRS. ZIMMER: Yes. The report is that 80 percent of women having their first baby were in labor less than four hours. This is compared with only 59 percent not using the suit who delivered by the end of four hours.

MRS. WALLACE: I think I cast my vote for a combination of natural childbirth training plus the birth suit.

DR. CHEAVENS: Mr. Wallace has a report on nutrition.

Nutrition During Pregnancy

MR. WALLACE: I've prepared this with the help of our obstetrician and my wife Nancy. And Nancy also is responsible for the handout on nutrition (the charts are reproduced at the end of this chapter).

Mineral and vitamin deficiencies have both been shown to have bad effects upon the unborn child. In some cases the results are poor bone formation such as results from rickets, due to lack of Vitamin D. A Harvard study of many mothers and babies showed that malnutrition resulted in an unusually large number of premature and still-births, extreme anemia, tuberculosis and rickets.[3]

One of the world's leading authorities on nutrition, Dr. Roger Williams, sums it up in his recent book this way, "Deformities, still births, retarded mental development, miscarriages and other more obscure troubles that show up in later life may have their origin in improper embryonic nutrition."[4]

Parents are eager for their children not only to be well and happy, but for them to mean as much as they can to the world they live in. There is some evidence that the right nutrition during pregnancy has something to do later with the child's measured intelligence. In one study pregnant women in slum areas were given extra vitamins to make sure they had enough, and, for purposes of comparison, an equal group of women in the same part of the city were studied who stayed on their normal diet, which did not have enough vitamins.[5]

This group on the poor diet were given placebos. These are pills or capsules containing a material that doesn't affect the body one way or another, but might help the woman's feelings, since many people feel better if they just take a pill, as some of us can testify. At the age of three, children of the mothers receiving vitamin supplements were 3.7 I.Q. points higher than the children whose mothers received no vitamin supplement. A year later the superior children were even more superior, reaching an average of 5.2 I.Q. points higher than the children of the mothers who did not have enough vitamins.

I know it's hard to believe, but in our land of superabundance of food, many people never have enough to eat, and many never have the right kinds of food. The fact that many women are on poor diets and without enough vitamins probably means that a great many babies will be born who will never be as bright as they would have been if the mother had been on a good diet. In this way the whole nation suffers. Think of this on a world-wide scale, and one can see why millions of people do not behave intelligently. The probable losses to the world due to this one factor may be beyond anything we have ever imagined.

A good many families have adequate incomes but the mother still does not have the right diet while carrying a child. About the only way to be sure of an adequate diet is to systematize it. It is really not much trouble to write out a number of menus including all the foods on a good recommended diet. There are a number of very interesting books on nutrition available, giving all the information anyone needs.[6] After making out a scheduled diet, to make doubly sure, one should check with the doctor.

During the gestation period the woman has two main problems about her eating. First, her intake of food should give her enough minerals and vitamins, and enough calories for her own vitality and for the best growth of the fetus. Second, it seems that most doctors agree that she should not put on too much weight.

One authority, R. E. Hall, suggests that to avoid becoming overweight, the expectant mother should practically do without sweets, fatty foods, and starches.[7] He also suggests a quart of milk a day, but reminds the reader that *skimmed* milk has all the protein, iron, and calcium that whole milk has. To get plenty of food and not gain too many pounds he also recommends eggs, cheese, lean meat, fruits, and vegetables.

A second authority, Ashley Montagu, suggests also a quart of milk, but less if American cheese (high in calcium) is also eaten.[8] He says that the diet should include leafy green and yellow vegetables, one or more servings a day. There should also be foods rich in Vitamin C, such as tomatoes and citrus fruits. Next come the important vitality foods with high protein content—eggs, fish, meat, poultry—one or more servings a day.

If one eats enough protein-content foods there won't be as much craving for sweets and starches as otherwise. This is true with children, too. Give them enough protein and they won't crave so much candy and sugar.

Montagu differs slightly from Hall in suggesting potatoes and bread, but recommending whole wheat or rye bread. Of course, we know that both bread, particularly some kinds, and potatoes are fattening and the needed foodstuff in them can also be found in nonfattening foods. So why not choose the nonfattening foods?

Montagu also includes salt and butter in moderation. But again —people are different and diets are individual affairs which should be tailored to the needs of the particular person. Women who are much overweight would certainly be on a different diet from those who are underweight. Some needs are common to all women such as foods with enough minerals and vitamins.

One of the most useful books was written for the American Dietetic Association.[9] The chapter on diet during pregnancy and lactation is to be highly recommended. The charts are taken from this reliable book.

Dr. Cheavens: Many people are shocked to find out that in our country so many pregnant women have no medical care at all prior to the birth of the baby. As was stated previously, recent statistics show that each year in 138 major cities in the United States there are around 445,000 expectant mothers who have no medical care at all prior to the birth of the baby.[10] This is one reason our country has a high infant mortality rate, and a high percentage of children who are defective at birth. This state of affairs need not exist.

Our next discussion will be on the most essential psychological ingredient in the life of a child.

FOOTNOTES

1. Ashley Montagu, *Life Before Birth* (New York: New American Library, Signet Books, 1965), pp. 103–113.

2. Ora Mendels, "A Revolution in Childbirth," *Ladies Home Journal*, Jan.–Feb. 1963, p. 40.

3. M. F. Ashley Montagu, "Constitutional and Prenatal Factors in Infant and Child Health," in *Symposium on the Healthy Personality*, ed. Milton J. E. Senn (New York: Josiah Macey, Jr., Foundation, 1950), pp. 148–75.

4. Roger J. Williams, *Nutrition in a Nutshell* (New York: Doubleday & Co., 1962), p. 1.

5. R. F. Harrell, et al., *The Effects of Mothers' Diets on the Intelligence of Offspring* (New York: Columbia University Press, 1955).

6. An excellent readable paperback book is Catharyn Elwood's *Feel Like a Million* (New York: Pocket Books, Inc., 1965).

7. R. E. Hall, *A Medical Guide for Pregnant Women* (New York: Bantam Books, 1965), pp. 42, 43.

8. Ashley Montagu, op. cit., p. 240.

9. Dorothea Turner, *Handbook of Diet Therapy* (Chicago: University of Chicago Press, 1965). The two charts that follow (on pages 40 and 41) are taken from pages 20 and 21 of this book and are used by permission of the publisher.

10. James C. Coleman, *Abnormal Psychology and Modern Life* (Chicago: Scott Foresman & Co., 1964), p. 523.

TABLE 1

NUTRIENT CONTENT OF DIET FOR USE DURING PREGNANCY AND LACTATION ‡‡
(Protein 82 Gm.; Calories 1,645–2,645)

DAILY FOOD INTAKE	QUANTITY		FOODSTUFFS				MINERALS		VITAMINS				
	Weight (Gm.)	Approximate Measure	CALORIES **	Protein (Gm.)	Fat (Gm.)	Carbohydrate (Gm.)	Ca (Mg.)	Fe (Mg.)	A (I.U.)	Ascorbic Acid (Mg.)	Thiamine (Mg.)	Riboflavin (Mg.)	Niacin (Mg.)
Milk, whole ††	976	1 quart	680	32	40	48	1,152	0.4	1,400	8	0.32	1.68	0.4
Egg	50	1 medium	75	7	5	......	27	1.1	590	......	0.05	0.15	Tr.
Meat, poultry, or fish, cooked *	120	4 oz. edible portion	300	28	20	......	16	3.4	35	......	0.40	0.25	5.9
Bread, whole-grain or enriched white †	150	5 slices	350	10	......	75	103	3.7	Tr.	......	0.37	0.25	3.2
Cereal, whole-grain or enriched white	20	½ cup	70	2	......	15	21	0.7	Tr.	......	0.07	0.05	0.7
Potato, cooked	100	1 small	70	2	......	15	5	0.5	Tr.	16	0.09	0.03	1.1
Vegetable (A) ‡	150	2 servings	20	1	......	4	43	1.2	2,180	32	0.10	0.10	0.9
Vegetable (B) §	50						12	0.5	1,660	5	0.03	0.03	0.4
Including green and yellow													
Fruit, citrus	100	1 serving	40			10	18	0.1	140	40	0.05	0.01	0.1
Fruit, other ‖		1 serving	40			10	7	0.4	473	5	0.02	0.03	0.4
Subtotal			1,645	82	65	177	1,404	12.0	6,478	106	1.50	2.58	13.1
Vitamin D concentrate ‡‡									660				
Separated fats and sweets ††			1,000										
Total §§			2,645	82			1,404	12.0§	7,138	106	1.50	2.58	13.1

* Estimate based on weekly consumption of 350 gm. poultry, 280 gm. beef, 280 gm. pork, 70 gm. fish, and 140 gm. poultry, *Meat Consumption Trends and Patterns* (U.S. Department of Agriculture, Agricultural Marketing Service, Agricultural Economics Division, Agriculture Handbook, No. 187 [Washington, D.C., July, 1960]).

† Each slice of bread has been considered to weigh 30 gm. (1 oz.) as in the values assigned to the exchange lists. It is recognized, however, that sliced bread may range between 20 and 30 gm. in weight. Adjustments should be made where usage varies.

‡ In making this estimate, it was considered that the commonly used vegetables A: tomatoes, snap beans, spinach, asparagus, broccoli, cabbage, lettuce, and cucumber, might be used 10 times weekly. Weighting was adapted from Agriculture Handbook, No. 215, *Consumption Trends and Patterns for Vegetables* (U.S. Department of Agriculture, Economic and Statistical Analysis Division, Economic Research Service [July, 1961]).

§ It was assumed that the most commonly used vegetables from the vegetable B group of the exchange lists were peas, carrots, beets, and squash. It was estimated that these vegetables might be used 4 times weekly averaging 50 gm. *Consump-*

nomic and Statistical Analysis Division, Economic Research Service [July, 1961]).

‖ Apples, bananas, canned peaches, pineapples, pears, apricots, and plums were considered commonly used. Weighting was adapted from *Consumption of Food in the United States*, Supplement for 1962 to Agriculture Handbook, No. 62 (U.S. Department of Agriculture, Agricultural Marketing Service [October, 1963]).

** Calories are rounded off to the nearest 5.

†† Per capita consumption of fats and sweets has been estimated as 2 oz. separated fat or oil and 3 oz. sugar daily. *National Food Situation, NFS-108* (U.S. Department of Agriculture, Economic Research Service [May, 1964]).

‡‡ 400–800 I.U. vitamin D may be obtained from fortified milk or a concentrate. During lactation 1½ quarts of milk should be used to provide extra protein and other nutrient levels proposed in the Recommended Dietary Allowances. The use of skim milk would reduce the calories in 1 quart by approximately 340.

§§ The total minerals, vitamins, and protein will approximate the recommended dietary allowances, with the exception of iron. Liver and other iron-rich foods may be used to augment this level. Caloric needs should be adjusted to

TABLE 2 *

MENU PATTERN AND SAMPLE MEALS DURING PREGNANCY AND LACTATION †
(82 Gm. Protein and 1,645–2,645 Calories; Derived from Table 1)

DAILY FOOD PLAN	SAMPLE MENU PATTERN	SAMPLE MEALS
	A.M.	
MILK GROUP		
1 qt. whole milk ⧣	1 citrus fruit or ½ cup juice	½ grapefruit
	½ cup cooked cereal or	¾ cup flakes with milk and sugar §
	¾ cup flake-type with milk and sugar §	1 slice toast with spread §
MEAT GROUP	1 slice enriched or whole-grain toast with spread §	Milk—1 glass
5 ounces or equivalent ‖	Milk—1 glass	
Cooked beef, pork, veal, lamb, poultry or fish		
	Noon	
VEGETABLE AND FRUIT GROUP	2 oz. meat, poultry, fish, cheese or 2 eggs ‖	Sandwich:
4 servings or more	Vegetable	2 slices meat
A dark-green or deep yellow vegetable daily for vitamin A value	2 slices enriched or whole-grain bread or substitute	2 slices bread
	Milk—1 glass	Sliced tomatoes and lettuce
A citrus fruit or other fruit rich in vitamin C daily		Milk—1 glass
	P.M.	
BREAD-CEREAL-POTATO-LEGUME GROUP	3 oz. meat, ‖ poultry, fish or substitute	Meat loaf
7 servings	½ cup potato or substitute	Baked potato
	Dark-green or deep-yellow vegetable	Asparagus tips
FATS AND SWEETS	Other vegetable	Cabbage slaw
	Fruit	Fresh strawberries
(Without this group the diet contains 1,645 calories)	2 slices enriched or whole-grain bread with spread § or substitute	2 hot rolls with spread §
10 teaspoons fat or oil contain 450 calories	Milk—1 glass	Milk—1 glass
10 teaspoons sugar, jelly, or honey contain 200 calories		
	Between	
Vitamin D ⧣	Milk—1 glass	Milk—1 glass

* The Recommended Dietary Allowances (Table 1) during pregnancy may be met by this pattern, with the exception of iron. Liver and other iron-rich foods may be used to augment this level.

† During lactation 1½ quarts of milk per day would provide the extra protein and other nutrients required to meet the Recommended Dietary Allowances.

§ 1 teaspoon sugar adds 20 calories; 1 teaspoon fat or oil adds 45 calories. Desserts like ice cream, pudding, and gelatin may add 150–300 calories. Adjustments in this group should be made to suit caloric needs of the individual patient.

‖ If additional meat is desired, one serving of the bread group (as 1 slice bread) may be omitted for each 1 oz. meat added, without changing the caloric value or reducing nutrient content. Other rearrangements or omissions should be assessed by reference to the values in Table 1.

⧣ The use of skim milk would reduce calories in 1 quart of milk by 360.

If 400 I.U. of vitamin D is not contained in 1 quart of milk a concentrate should be prescribed.

5. The Advantage to Your Child of an Abundance of Love

DR. CHEAVENS: The one most important ingredient in the early social and emotional development of the infant is maternal love. The mother's affectionate attitude is shown by the way she handles the baby, by her voice, and in dozens of small and sometimes subtle ways.

Of all the psychological threats which may hang over the head of any infant, one stands out as more serious in its consequences than any other. This is the threat of being deprived of love by the mother, or the mother-substitute. This denial of affection by the mother may show itself in neglect of the young child or in open rejection. Sometimes the infant is deprived by unavoidable separation, as in the serious illness or death of the mother.

By the same token, of all the promises extended by life to the infant, none can compare with the promise of a warm, close companionship with the mother. If the companionship continues long enough, the child usually develops a strength and resilience of personality, and a capacity for establishing close, satisfying ties with other people that will fill life with richness and meaning.

We have all known children who grew up experiencing hardships but who also experienced an abundance of love in the family. The love offsets the hardships. Usually these children come to be people who have good friends, and who generally do well in life.

For the infant to develop normally, he needs consistent love from the mother shown by ample physical contact. Much of this contact occurs during feeding, changing, and bathing, but also a great deal of it when the mother is playing with the baby or merely enjoying holding him.

Mrs. Dana, who has six very healthy, individualistic boys, has some very definite ideas about the relationship of mother and infant during feeding. Our first report will be hers. She also belongs to an interesting organization about which she will tell you.

Affectionate Contact During Feeding

MRS. DANA: One easy and natural method of pleasant contact for both child and mother is breast-feeding. Among pediatricians there is rather general agreement that breast-feeding is better than bottle-feeding for the baby. The attitude of modern medicine toward breast-feeding is well summarized in an article by Dr. Frank H. Richardson, an authority on the subject. He states that ". . . it is still almost universally accepted by doctors and especially researchers, that natural feeding is superior to artificial. Increased antibody immunity protection is only one of several important factors." [1]

He cites two other authorities, Dr. Paul Gyorgy, professor of pediatrics of the University of Pennsylvania, and Dr. Waldo E. Nelson, professor of pediatrics at the Temple University School of Medicine, who state that infants who are breast-fed are more immune to disease than the bottle-fed. Immunity against intestinal disorders, respiratory diseases, and infections of the middle ear are specifically named.

Dr. Richardson goes on to say that, in addition to the nutritional benefits, there are undeniable psychological benefits which accrue to both mother and child from the intimate contact.

I think I ought to say here that not all the experts agree with Dr. Richardson. One very good book Mrs. Sonneman lent me states that infants can thrive on artificial milk and that it is now impossible to demonstrate any clear health advantage from breast-feeding.[2] Of course the formulas have been greatly improved in the last few years. Maybe the greatest advantage of breast feeding lies in the close relationship between mother and child.

This leads me to insert a word about the organization I belong to, La Leche League. Those of you who know Spanish recognize *leche* as the word for milk. A large number of mothers have organized La Leche League to teach mothers not only the benefits to baby and mother from breast-feeding, but how to succeed at it. Their very instructive book is available in a paperback edition.[3]

Of course, if the infant must be bottle-fed, the time of feeding can be one of affectionate contact. The mother's speech to the child can be soft and pleasing. She can show affection through caresses and by the way the infant is held during feeding. I'm not an extremist on this subject at all, you see. With either way of feeding the mother can show affection.

MRS. KASTLY: If the mother breast-feeds the baby, what do we know about the length of time this should continue and the best weaning practice?

MRS. DANA: Perhaps Dr. Cheavens would like to answer that.

DR. CHEAVENS: The picture isn't too clear. One of the best studies shows there were fewer emotional upsets if weaning took place between five and eleven months.[4] Long-delayed weaning has shown no real advantages. It is rather widely agreed that weaning should be gradual and gentle.

MRS. DANA: Like some of the mothers who take natural child-birth training and become fanatical advocates, our organization has some extremists. Not withstanding these few, it is a good organization promoting something that I feel means greater happiness for both mother and child.

DR. CHEAVENS: We see that the pleasurable contact of mother and child during feeding is one way both may learn to express love. People can learn to love, and learn how to love. Dr. Erich Fromm has a helpful book called the *Art of Loving* [5] in which he gives pointers on learning how to love. If the mother feels she is somewhat deficient in love, she can learn to love more. Let us look for a few minutes at the results of being deprived of love.

The Penalties of Lack of Affection

If the baby does not have consistent maternal contact, development is nearly always subnormal in all areas of personality. Intelligence usually does not increase as it should. The child does not do well in his social relationships. The development of conscience is often twisted or weak. The infant starved for love is lacking in physical vitality and strength, and has less resistance to disease. The death-rate of infants deprived of maternal affection is distinctly higher than the death-rate of those who have had a plentiful supply of love.

Many people think that if an infant is supplied with protection from contagious or infectious disease, given an ample diet, and provided with warmth and shelter, he ought to thrive. Such is not the case. Spitz, a medical investigator, studied four groups of children.[6] Three groups lived with their own mothers. The other group, comprised of sixty-one children, lived in a public institution. The physical needs of the institutional group were well taken care of. Only the psychological needs were unfulfilled. There were too many babies for each nurse. This meant the babies could not receive enough mothering. At the time in that particular institution there was nothing that could be done to remedy this.

The babies were given a Developmental Quotient (D.Q.) test on which scores from 90 to 110 are average. This test shows how far the baby has gone toward normal development in many ways. To begin with, the institutionalized children had an average D.Q. of 124, the second highest of the four. Following a year of institutional life and not enough maternal contacts, their D.Q. had dropped to 72. In the other three groups, none of whom lived under what could be called ideal conditions but all of whom received at least average amounts of affection, there were no such tragic losses in D.Q. We are so in the habit of thinking in terms of mere physical needs, that finding out about these sad results from unfilled social and emotional needs comes as a shock to most of us.

In a follow-up study a year later, it was discovered that the same sort of thing had continued, but with a very high death rate among the institutionalized children. They were retarded in height, in weight, in standing, in walking, and in talking. By the end of the second year the D.Q. of the emotionally deprived children had dropped to 45.[7] Such losses are nothing short of disastrous.

Wolf, another medical researcher, studied the Developmental Quotients of 118 babies in several institutions and found out how much maternal care had been given the infants. After the age of three months, differences between those receiving enough maternal care and those who did not have enough began to show up. After eight months the deprived infants were so disturbed emotionally that the doctors could not even test them.[8]

Our next report is from Mr. Victor.

MR. VICTOR: I was shocked to learn from my reading what happens when a young child is deprived of maternal affection. One of the best studies along this line was made by Dr. W. Goldfarb, director of the Henry Ittleson Center of Child Research, who compared two groups of adolescents.[9] All the children in one group, at around four months of age had been placed in an institution, where they had spent about three years before being adopted. All the children in the second group had been placed directly in foster homes from their own homes. The institutionalized children had not received much mothering. It seems that the other group had received at least an average amount.

The institutionalized group showed below normal development in every area of personality. They were indifferent, apathetic and lacking in drive toward definite goals. They were below par socially, being unable to form satisfactory relationships with other people, either children or adults. The children placed directly in foster homes had developed normally in all of these areas.

The clearest difference was in measured intelligence. The children who had not been in institutions were average in intelligence, while not a single child who had lived in an institution scored as high as an I.Q. of 100; their average came out at only I.Q. 68, which is usually classified as mental deficiency.

One authority in this field has written a fine book—*Maternal Care and Mental Health*. Dr. John Bowlby, director of the Child Guidance Department of the Travistock Clinic in London, and consultant in mental health for the World Health Organization, has gathered a great amount of evidence of this kind, and nearly all of it is in agreement. His evidence should convince the worst doubters. Bowlby says: "The extent to which these studies, undertaken by people of many nations, varied training, and as often as not, ignorant of each other's conclusions, confirm and support each other, is impressive. What each individual piece of work lacks in thoroughness, scientific reliability or precision is largely made good by the concordance of the whole. Nothing in scientific method carries more weight than this."[10]

DR. CHEAVENS: While I value Dr. Bowlby's book highly, a great deal of the investigation reported in it is not as scientific as it should be. But it stimulated others to do more careful scientific work along the same lines. This more recent and better work may be found summarized in the review of child development research published by the Russell Sage Foundation.[11] The report of this summary does not change the general conclusion that maternal deprivation has serious consequences on infants. Good substitute mothering offsets this to a great degree.

The relationship of mother to child prior to separation is a factor. If the relationship has not been good, damage has already been done, and damage due to separation is not as noticeable.

The Effects of Short Separations

Even the best-informed parents are not often aware of what even a short separation from the mother can do to a child before he is five. A separation of only a few days may prove to be very disturbing.

One young couple took care of this problem with both their children when they were babies by letting them have frequent contacts with grandparents and an aunt until they felt safe and happy with them in the parents' absence. Whenever this couple had to be separated from their children, they left them in the care of a mother-substitute with whom they felt secure and comfortable. This is the right way to do it.

To those who would like to do further reading about this I recommend the book mentioned by Mr. Victor: *Maternal Care and Mental Health* by J. Bowlby, and the Russell Sage Foundation book I mentioned earlier, both of which contain good digests of all the studies related to these important questions. About the problems connected with short separations, Bowlby gives an unpublished report made by doctors Burlingham and Anna Freud during World War II, when the two psychiatrists were in charge of a residential nursery at Hampstead, England. They were trying to make separations of children from their mothers easier by slow stages. This seemed to make the shock less serious for children over three years of age, but for those younger it did not.

The two psychiatrists said: "Infants of that age [1½ to 2½] can stand sudden changes and separations of a day's length without any visible effect. Whenever it is more than that, they tend to lose their emotional ties, revert in their instincts and regress in their behavior."[12]

When the mother returned after an absence of only a few days, the children might show any of a number of signs, such as anger and hostility toward the mother. Sometimes they wanted too much attention. Some of the children did not want to have anything to do with anybody. They withdrew completely and did not seem to care about anything. They had lost hope. Other children after short separations would take up with just anyone. But such superficial relationships did not mean very much.

Perhaps one reason why so many of the experts in this field are not alert to the danger of separations is that often the infant does the best he can by making these shallow attachments to almost any adult. These can be mistaken for a good adjustment. Or in other cases, the baby has become hopeless and does not have much life, but is judged to be a "good" baby, when really he is severely depressed.

We still do not have enough evidence about the possible damage of short separations to the very young. We need many carefully controlled studies so that pediatricians, child psychologists, nurses, and others having contact with parents can give them accurate, reliable information.

But, in the light of what evidence we have, most parents should be very cautious about even short periods of separation and alert to possible damage to the young child. In case such separations are necessary, the right precautions can be taken to help offset emotional shock. The child should always be left in the care of someone with whom he feels secure and happy.

Many parents are careless about their baby-sitters. The least that should be done is to make sure the person is reliable and has affection for children. The children should become familiar with the sitter and come to feel safe and comfortable with her before they are left alone with her. Even with a kindly, competent person, the child may suffer considerable trauma if there has been no previous opportunity to make friends.

It seems that after most children are five years old they are not hurt as much by separations from the mother as they are at an earlier age.[13] It looks as if the child develops some sort of strength to resist the shock of parental absence. Of course children need an abundance of love and companionship with parents at all ages.

If an infant has had a happy relationship with the mother, and a separation takes place, extra mothering from a good mother-substitute will help to cut down on the ill effects. However, even if the mother-substitute is a good one, the infant sometimes will reject her entirely. This is much less likely to happen if the substitute is brought in from time to time and associated with both mother and infant before separation takes place. As we said before, if the substitute is one with whom the child is familiar and feels secure, the absence may have no ill effects at all.

It is easy to see why this business of both long and short separations is so important. I'm sure we all know well-meaning parents who have taken trips and left their infant in the care of someone who had a reputation of being a good baby-sitter but who was a complete stranger to the child. I know a couple who did this and were shocked on their return when the child would have nothing to do with them at first. It took some time and a great deal of patience and understanding before the child again began to show she loved them.

You may be wondering as I am why separations should be so damaging to the child. I don't think we know all the answers, but we have some interesting clues. All living things learn. We have some experiments that show that even the unborn baby can be conditioned, which is learning on the simplest level.

Along this line, Mrs. Sonneman will share with us a report which she wrote while working on her master's degree in child psychology.

*Conditioning of the Infant to the Mother's Heartbeat**

MRS. SONNEMAN: One thing the unborn child is conditioned to is the beat of the mother's heart. Psychologist Lee Salk of the City Hospital at Elmhurst, New York, designed an ingenious series of experiments based upon this prenatal conditioning.[14] He used 102 babies for the experiment and a matched group for controls. Dr. Salk had a recording made with nothing on it but the sound of a mother's heartbeat—72 paired beats per minute. He played this record to the experimental babies for four days and nights. The infants in the control group were not exposed to the sound, but in all other ways they received the same treatment as the experimental infants.

The experimental infants gained more weight in this period than the control infants, and both groups ate the same amount and kind of food. It looks as if the experimental babies digested and assimilated their food better.

The amount of crying for both groups was carefully measured. The experimental babies cried about half as much as the control babies. This would seem to indicate that those exposed to the sound of the maternal heartbeat were more relaxed than those who were not exposed to it. Dr. Salk interprets the results as indicating that the sound of the maternal heartbeat reduces anxiety in the infants who hear it.

Experiments were also carried out on a group of 26 other children, ranging in age from 16 months to 37 months. They were observed under four different kinds of conditions as they dropped off to sleep—exposed to the reproduced sound of the recorded heartbeat; exposed to a metronome giving off 72 beats per minute; exposed to recorded lullabies; and no exposure to any of the sounds named above.

Under each condition, the children were carefully watched to find out how long it took them to go to sleep. There were no differences in the average time for dropping off to sleep under exposure to the metronome, or to lullabies, or when there were no experimental sounds at all. But under exposure to the recording of the mother's heartbeat, the children averaged falling asleep in one-half the time required by the other three groups, again giving strong evidence that the heartbeat sound cuts down on anxiety and causes the child to relax. The fact that neither the metronome, with the same number of beats as the mother's heart, nor the rhythm

* This report was written by Mrs. Sonneman.

of the lullabies made any difference, shows that there probably is something special in the recorded maternal heartbeat.

The experimenters also observed the way 287 mothers carried their babies. Around 80 percent of both the right-handed and the left-handed mothers carried their babies with the head on the left side close to the rhythm of the heartbeat. The mothers did this automatically and were not aware of it. When women were observed carrying grocery packages, about 50 percent carried them on the right side and about 50 percent on the left. The mothers automatically carried their babies differently from other things.

From this series of experiments we can see one likely reason for the great need of babies for close bodily contacts with the mother. During the long period of physical dependence of the unborn baby upon the mother, the baby gets accustomed to the rhythm of her heartbeat which is associated with security. After birth, when the baby is held by its mother, it senses the rhythm of the heartbeat and again feels safe.

During the nine months before birth the baby is also surrounded by fluid. Its skin is gently stimulated by the contact. After birth it is reasonable to believe that gentle contact such as being held or caressed would increase the baby's feeling of comfort and security.

FOOTNOTES

1. F. H. Richardson, M.D., "Breast or Bottle Feeding?" *Today's Health*, May 1962, p. 65.

2. Benjamin T. Burton, ed., *The Heinz Handbook of Nutrition*, 2nd ed. (New York: McGraw-Hill, 1965), p. 163.

3. *The Womanly Art of Breast Feeding* (Franklin Park, Ill. [3332 Rost St.]: La Leche League International, Inc.).

4. R. R. Sears, E. E. Maccoby, and H. Levin. *Patterns of Child Rearing* (Evanston, Ill.: Row, Peterson, 1957).

5. Erich Fromm, *The Art of Loving* (New York: Harper & Row, 1956).

6. R. A. Spitz, "Hospitalism, an Inquiry into the Genesis of Psychiatric Conditions in Early Childhood," in *Psychoanalytic Study of the Child*, vol. 1, R. S. Eissler, et al., eds. (New York: International Universities Press, 1945), pp. 53–74.

7. R. A. Spitz, "Hospitalism, a Follow-up Report on Investigation Described in Vol. 1, 1945," in *Psychoanalytic Study of the Child*, vol. 2,

R. S. Eissler, et al., eds. (New York: International Universities Press, 1946), pp. 113–17.

8. J. Bowlby, *Maternal Care and Mental Health* (Geneva: World Health Organization, 1955), p. 17.

9. W. Goldfarb, "The Effects of Early Institutional Care on Adolescent Personality," *Journal of Experimental Education* 12 (1943), 106–29.

10. Bowlby, p. 15.

11. Martin L. and Lois W. Hoffman, eds., *Child Development Research*, vol. 1 (New York: The Russell Sage Foundation, 1964), pp. 95–117.

12. Bowlby, pp. 24–26.

13. Ibid., p. 21.

14. L. Salk, "Mother's Heartbeat as an Imprinting Stimulus," *Transactions* of the New York Academy of Sciences, s. 3, vol. 24, no. 7 (1962), pp. 753–63.

6. Advantages of Balance in Child-Rearing

MR. SHELBY: I recognize the importance of love for children but aren't there lots of other important things in child-rearing? A child has a variety of needs besides just a demonstration of love. What are these other attitudes and practices that mean a child will have his best chance?

Frustration vs. Overprotection

DR. CHEAVENS: John is right. All of us who are parents know how many-sided and complicated the whole process of raising children is. I think I'll try to sum it up under the heading of balance. There is a golden mean which the intelligent parent strives for. Our future meetings will take up many of the various parts to giving the child his best chance.

Children must be exposed to life as it exists according to their ability and stages of maturation. Someone has said that if the parent's back yard is smooth he should dig some holes in it. If things are made too smooth and easy for a child, he does not learn to cope with his problems. Having problems is essential to problem-solving. Today the person who does not learn to solve all kinds of problems is drastically penalized. If the child is to develop resourcefulness and courage in facing his world, he must be exposed to the world.

You will recognize that at every stage of development there are problems which are beyond the child's ability. The toddler is too young to learn to cross a busy street safely. The four-year-old cannot prepare a well-balanced meal—this is an adult level problem. But as the child reaches the stage when he can solve problems on his own level, he should be exposed to them.

Not long ago I saw a very acceptable wooden boat built by a four-year-old out of blocks of wood. He had done the sawing and the nailing and the painting. Yet I know a mother who will never let her four-year-old have a hammer, because he might mash his finger. And of course he will! But from this he will learn to hammer more accurately. In the case of the boat-building boy, his father had taught him how to saw effectively with a small saw and then turned him loose with the materials.

Overprotection can be of two types as pointed out by Dr. David M. Levy in his book, *Maternal Over-Protection.*[1] One of these shows itself by the parent's dominating the child. The child is not allowed to grow up. His decisions are all made for him. The second type manifests itself in overindulgence. The child always gets what he wants, even at the expense of others, and does not mature socially and emotionally.

Under the dominating, oversupervising parent the child may be outwardly submissive and compliant, but usually there is a great deal of suppressed rebellion. With the overindulgent parent who nearly always lets the child have his way, the child becomes demanding, selfish, and blind to the feelings and needs of others. In any case the child's personality development becomes distorted or otherwise damaged. Some parents change from domination to overindulgence from one minute to the next.

MR. INMAN: Some parents feel that modern child psychologists teach that a child should never be inhibited or taught to suppress himself. What do you say to that?

MRS. SONNEMAN: I'd like to speak to that. In all of my recent reading in child psychology I haven't found any expert that would take that stand.

DR. CHEAVENS: I agree. One of the surest ways to produce an insecure child is for the parent to set no limitations to his behavior. Anything goes! Most children under such circumstances will try to get the parent to set up some limitations on behavior. Every child must learn, if he is to lead a satisfying life, that there are many things he wishes to do that he may not do, and other things that he does not want to do, that he must do. Self-discipline has always been, and is now, essential in our world. Otherwise you have nothing but anarchy.

Here again we seek the golden mean. Out of many homes come overinhibited children, doomed for unhappy living. Out of many other homes come children who have no inner controls at all, causing themselves and others constant trouble.

One way of showing love is to teach the child realistically that, in this world, some things may not be done, other things must be done. Not very long ago a shocking crime was committed in a community not far from here. It was particularly puzzling to me because nowhere in the background of this young man who was guilty did there seem to be a history of behavior that would later become criminality. I finally picked up one fact which might be a clue to his personality formation and help explain what he did. A neighbor, in commenting on the young man and his parents, said, "He never asked for anything that he didn't get." If this is true, what were the parents thinking of when they made him feel that every desire of his would be granted? That would be like constructing a high-powered car without any brakes! Yet many parents deal with their children on this basis.

So we see there are dangers to personality development which later may become dangers to society from neglecting to teach a child the limitations to his behavior.

Of course there are many ways of showing the child what the limitations on his behavior are. Usually children, even very young ones, want their parents to explain things, to give reasons. I have found that even when a child was too young to understand the reasons, he seemed to like my giving them, as if by my explanation I was showing consideration and respect for him, and that I was on his side. This made our relations better, and promoted cooperation.

MRS. WALLACE: What are the causes of a parent's overindulging a child?

MRS. VICTOR: I suppose a personal confession would be in order here. I know I have overindulged both of my boys. I had so many outside activities in which I was interested that I turned the boys over to a maid. Well, I felt guilty about my neglect. When they asked me for something they didn't need, this guilt made me as weak as water and I would give in, knowing I shouldn't. But since these discussions started I've been giving my boys real companionship for most of the day and I am getting stronger in doing what I know is good for them. I'm no longer afraid to say no.

MR. WALLACE: I can see how that would work. But with some parents isn't it just less trouble to give in? They want to save themselves trouble.

MRS. VICTOR: I think that's right, but again I'd like to admit that I also was overprotective and I think my guilt about neglecting the boys was behind that. I was trying to convince myself that I really was on my boys' side and so I tried to overshelter them. I don't think that's the only reason for overprotection, though.

MRS. ZIMMER: Some parents are just worriers and are always expecting the worst. They're overprotective.

MR. INMAN: We have neighbors who have a child with cerebral palsy. They've had a hard fight to keep from overprotecting their son. I think parents of any child with a special weakness or deficiency might be both overprotective and overindulgent. The result in any case would be a rotten kid. A child with a deficiency has to learn that he can't have his way all the time, just like any normal child. And he's got to learn as much independence as possible, too.

DR. CHEAVENS: I recall one study indicating that 64 percent of 80 orthopedically handicapped children had been overprotected by parents, resulting in their immature emotional and social behavior.[2]

This brings up our next topic of discussion: What is the relation of the way we rear our children to their self-concepts?

Balance and Self-Concept

DR. CHEAVENS: Each person defines himself. This definition of himself is generally called self-concept. He has attitudes toward himself and ideas about himself. He may have differing attitudes toward the various sides of his personality. He may see himself as superior intellectually but inferior in mechanical aptitude. He may see himself as socially skilled but inadequate in athletics. Self-concept is what the person thinks of himself, accurate or inaccurate, real or imagined.

Perhaps central in self-concept is whether or not the person sees himself as a person of worth, as deserving of affection and respect. This attitude of self-respect, a feeling of worth, is not necessarily a matter of how much ability the person has or how much he has achieved. Many people with limited abilities and no noteworthy achievement may still have a concept of themselves as people worthy of the love and the respect of others. Those who have worked much with the mentally retarded can testify to such positive self-concept on the part of some of those who know they are below par in their ability to think and to achieve.

Others with superior minds, a large list of outstanding skills

and a record of notable achievement may have very little feeling of
worth or self-respect and may conceive of themselves as utterly
unlovable and worthless. Suicide and attempted suicide are often
symptoms of a deep feeling of unworthiness and a lack of self-
esteem. Some people of high intelligence and outstanding achievements commit suicide.

MR. VICTOR: I remember reading in the autobiography of
Anton Boisen, who became seriously mentally ill, that one of the
underlying causes of his illness was what he called "a catastrophic
loss of self-respect."[3] A feeling of self-respect is one of the big
parts of a person's mental and emotional health.

MRS. WALLACE: How does a child develop his self-concept?

MRS. SONNEMAN: You learn it from those you live closest to.
In the beginning, the most important people in the child's life and
the ones he is closest to are the parents.

The affection of the parents gradually creates a feeling in the
child that he is worthy of love. The respect of the parents for the
child as a person brings a response of respect for the parents from
the child. And if the parents respect him, he begins to respect
himself.

If the parents do not love him, this causes the child to feel he
is unlovable and unworthy. Belittling the child and his abilities is
the beginning of the child's feeling that he cannot do anything
very well. He begins to have strong feelings of inferiority. If the
parents keep getting angry at the child, it gives the child the
feeling and the idea that he is a terrible person and guilty of
awful things, when usually he has made only some small mistake.

MRS. SHELBY: It seems that any handicapped child would have
a hard time developing a good self-concept.

DR. CHEAVENS: But if the handicapped child is loved he feels
that he's a lovable person. If his parents don't overprotect him but
let him solve his own problems as much as possible, he begins to
feel that he can cope with his environment, and he develops a
feeling of both self-respect and self-confidence.

MRS. DANA: I have an acquaintance whose cousin shows both
sides of the picture. This young man, George R., was recently
helped by the state's Department of Vocational Rehabilitation. As
a child he had a severe loss in hearing that cut off many opportunities of learning. He could not keep up in school because of bad
hearing. And nobody did anything about his deafness. This defect
was still pronounced in adulthood, when his measured I.Q. was
around 80. It showed him to be a backward person and a slow
learner.

His parents, while treating him kindly, had always given him the feeling that he could not do even the simplest job well. Then, as an adult, he went to live with a cousin who had a small routine job of painting to be done. His cousin invited George to help.

George said, "I can't do that."

"There's nothing to it," explained his cousin. "You just dip the roller in the paint and roll it on."

Still George demurred saying, "My father told me I couldn't do work like that. I haven't ever done things like that."

When finally he was persuaded to try the job, he caught on quickly, did good work, and was proud of it. This was the beginning of a change in his self-concept.

His cousin helped George get in touch with the rehabilitation workers, who found out he could be trained in cabinet work. Now he owns his own shop, is saving his money and takes a great deal of pride in his achievement. In his case, the development of a skill helped change his self-concept. But more important was the fact that his cousin thought he was worth something, and that he could learn to make his own living.

DR. CHEAVENS: From Mrs. Dana's example, we see the damage to self-concept from parents. We also see that a certain amount of this damage can be repaired by friends or relatives who have confidence in the handicapped person. Experiences of success can improve anybody's self-concept.

Self-Concept and Behavior

To realize how much the self-concept means, all we need to do is look at ourselves and see the way we get along every day. On a very basic level, I have a concept of myself as a swimmer. I know I have only average speed for short distances. I know that if I swim slowly on my back I can hold out for fairly long distances if I have to, but it would take some sort of emergency for this to happen. So I don't go in for swimming races. I don't try to swim the English Channel. My self-concept of myself as a swimmer has a great deal to do with my decisions about swimming. I swim for fun and I feel considerable security around the water.

A young woman I know married before finishing college. She recently took two extra college courses that nobody made her take. She wanted to take them. She would never have enrolled for them at all unless she had seen herself as a person who could succeed in learning difficult subject matter.

I also know a young man who put together a huge, complicated loader for pulpwood. He saw himself as a person of considerable mechanical ingenuity and ability or he never would have attempted the job. That he succeeded in his effort was indicated by a recently published article about how he made his loader.

In each case self-concept had much to do with what the person was willing to try. I do not see myself as a person of mechanical inventiveness and skill, so I do not tackle a job like designing and constructing a complicated mechanism. Much of any person's choices and his courses of action are determined by self-concept. The child who has grown up feeling he is a person worthy of love and respect will approach other people with confidence, feeling he will gain their love and respect. The child who learns early that he can work through problems will not be afraid to tackle problems and solve them.

For those of you that are interested in the scientific approach to the subject, Mrs. Kastly has volunteered to bring us a brief report.

Self-Concept and Personality Development

MRS. KASTLY: I am summarizing several studies in which different tests were used that have helped me to understand better the importance of a healthy self-concept. In one of these, 300 boys and girls were examined in the fourth, fifth, and sixth grades.[4] The investigators found that children with a poor self-concept were much more anxious than children with a good self-concept.

Using 100 college students, another similar project verified that there was close relationship between a poor self-concept and a great deal of anxiety.[5] Two other investigators found that poor self-concept was closely related to poor adjustment in general and that those having a satisfactory self-concept were much better adjusted.[6]

Preschool children have been given opportunities for social contacts to increase social self-confidence, and others in the same school were given training in play skills. These activities raised the child's self-concept.[7] I might add that case studies show that overprotection and oversupervision are damaging to self-concept. The child senses that the parent has little confidence in him, and he then doubts his own abilities.

MRS. WALLACE: What are the ways for improving one's self-concept, since it is so important?

Ways of Improving Self-Concept

DR. CHEAVENS: Dr. Carl R. Rogers, who was not long ago professor of psychotherapy at the University of Wisconsin School of Medicine and is now on the staff of the Western Behavioral Sciences Institute of La Jolla, California, found that people having a low self-concept were a great deal more maladjusted than people who had a high self-concept.[8] There was considerably more unhappiness and tension on the part of those with a low self-concept. The major aim of Roger's study was to find out any changes brought about by Roger's method in counseling. Evidence showed that counseling brought about a great deal of improvement in self-concept. There was some change toward the person's being more realistic in what he thought about himself. That is, the person shifted in the direction of more down-to-earth, reachable goals for himself, rather than his former unrealistic level of ambition. But he also shifted in the direction of having more self-respect and thinking of himself as a worthy person.

While counseling may bring about betterment of self-concept, it is uphill, time-consuming work. There is a lack of skilled counselors and therapists to do the job. We do not have enough therapists to minister even to the seriously mentally ill, much less to those who are unhappy, rather than ill, who are living in dissatisfaction and too much tension.

I am glad to say there are other ways of improving one's self-concept. A person who has any sort of small success due to his own effort may begin to have a better opinion of himself. Any improvement, no matter how small, is worth working for. And even some small success usually gets recognition from others. This recognition improves self-concept.

In our country those who have felt unloved and rejected in early childhood are those who have suffered the worst damage. With them, whatever gains that can be made should be made. Many of them will become parents and will find it hard to relate well to their own children. This in turn will damage the self-concept of the children.

Of course, as we have said, the parents are not the only ones who influence the self-concept of the child. There are often others in his life who make him feel he is a person of worth, even if his parents do not. Relatives, neighbors, friends, the child's own playmates may all have a part in this.

The Need for Parent-Education

One of our greatest needs today is for parent-education. Many parents feel this need and organize informal study groups. In San Antonio many years ago, two neighborhoods formed groups like this with about thirty parents in each group. The membership of the groups would gradually change, but these two informal discussion groups continued over a very long period of time, helping to fill the need of parents to exchange ideas, books, and to talk about their common problems. The members of these groups were enthusiastic in their praise of their friendly meetings where they all received help about many different family problems.

Many churches organize groups of young parents for study and discussion of problems in child-rearing. The Parent-Teacher Associations have done a great work in parent education. But whatever the source, parent education is one of our most positive forces for bringing parents to constructive attitudes and practices that will give their children the best chances for positive personality development. These discussions are good examples of what should be going on everywhere.

FOOTNOTES

1. David M. Levy, *Maternal Over-Protection* (New York: University Press, 1957), p. 35.

2. R. C. Kemmerer, "An exploratory psychological study of crippled children," *Psychological Record* 4, (1940), 47–100.

3. Anton T. Boisen, *Exploration of the Inner World* (Chicago: Willet, Clark and Company, 1936).

4. L. P. Lipsitt, "Self-Concept Scale for Children and Its Relationship to the Children's Form of the Manifest Anxiety Scale," *Child Development* 29 (1958), 463–72.

5. J. V. Mitchell, Jr., "Goal-setting Behavior as a Function of Self-acceptance, Over- and Under-achievement, and Related Personality Variables," *Journal of Educational Psychology* 50 (1959), 93–104.

6. V. J. Crandall and U. Belluzi, "Some Relationships of Interpersonal and Intrapersonal Conceptualizations to Personal-Social Adjustment," *Journal of Personality* 23 (1954), 224–32.

7. L. M. Jack, "An experimental study of ascendant behavior in pre-school children," *University of Iowa Studies in Child Welfare* 9 (1934), 7–65.

8. Carl R. Rogers, *On Becoming a Person* (Boston: Houghton-Mifflin, 1961), pp. 256–58.

7. Advantages of
   Rich and Varied Experiences

DR. CHEAVENS: When we were discussing the formation of self-concept, it became clear that the child needs to have many positive experiences of all kinds in order that he may find out what he can learn and what he can achieve. Childhood should be a time of rich and varied experiences, not only for the formation of his self-concept, but for the optimal development of every facet of his life.

A few years ago I took my two-year-old friend Carolyn on a brief walk into a wooded area close to where she lives. We visited a little creek toward the back of the area and perhaps for the first time Carolyn learned to say "creek." She was seeing and exploring the creek and learning the word for the experience at the same time. We also saw schools of silvery minnows in the creek and she was entranced. She learned to say the word "minnow" and repeated it with delight as she watched them flash through the clear water. This was a simple experience but priceless!

Life is interesting because of such experiences. And words are fun—fun to learn, and fun to repeat. The foundation is being laid for the thinking process. The storehouse of pleasant memory begins to be filled. Carolyn talked with me about that experience many times after that.

Language development is largely dependent upon experience. The experience comes first and is followed by the words that name the experience and describe it. Sensory development and discrimination are also largely dependent upon experience. Readiness for reading, which in turn is related to the earlier speaking vocabulary, is also greatly dependent upon experience. Carolyn is now, at age five, beginning to learn to read and the process seems natural and almost spontaneous. Her younger brother is also beginning to recognize a number of printed words. The major reason for this, aside from their innate capacity, is that their lives have been rich in experience, which has been followed by concept formation and by the spoken word that names the concept. The next step after learning the spoken word is the recognition of the written word.

All learning, at least as far as we now know, comes through the avenues of our various senses, with sight and hearing the two main avenues. Sensory experience is the way we learn to tell the difference between objects as well as their similarities. We learn to discriminate and to generalize through our senses. You can see why rich and varied experiences are necessary for the child.

The following reports were chosen from a number of topics we thought would be interesting. Mr. Wallace, who seems to be gifted as an animal trainer, selected a topic having to do with restricting the sensory experiences of animals.

Penalties of Restricted Experience in Animals

MR. WALLACE: The first part of my report deals with animals I'm not too fond of—rats. One group of young rats was raised in cages with certain geometric figures painted in black on the walls. Another group had walls that were blank.

Later the experimenters taught the mature rats tasks that involved telling the difference between these geometric figures. The group that had the figures painted on the walls of the cages learned to discriminate faster than the group that had blank walls.[1] The mere early exposure gave the advantage. So, if you want your child to learn algebra, buy wallpaper with algebraic symbols. (This statement was rewarded with laughter by the group.)

Since we don't let experimenters use our children in experiments of sensory deprivation, they are forced to use animals. Chimpanzees born with normal vision but reared in darkness are definitely subnormal in object avoidance when they are later exposed to light. That is, the chimp runs into objects when he's looking right at them! This deficit lasts for a long time after the chimps are exposed to normal lighting, and the effects are very hard to overcome.[2]

The same sort of thing applies to rats reared in darkness. Experimenters have also deprived young chimps of early experiences of touch by putting cardboard cuffs on their hands and feet. When these chimps matured and the cuffs were removed, the experimenters found that it was almost impossible for the chimps to learn by the sense of touch. Yet chimps reared without the cuffs could learn these tasks quite readily. The experimental animals never completely overcame this handicap.[3] Some of the setbacks seemed to be irreversible.

DR. CHEAVENS: Mrs. Zimmer had already done some reading on the next topic which influenced her to choose it.

Sensory Deprivation in Humans

MRS. ZIMMER: While we don't have experiments with children, you too may have read about the experiments with adults. Brief periods of social isolation, accompanied by reduction of sensory stimuli, seem to have a bad effect on how a human being functions. In one of these experiments [4] male college students lay on a comfortable bed twenty-four hours a day as long as they could stand it. This was usually from about two to three days. They wore goggles that let light in but prevented clear sight of objects. They wore cotton gloves and cardboard cuffs limiting their experiences of touch. They lay on foam rubber pillows. The cubicle to which they were confined was "semi-soundproof," limiting experiences of hearing. However, two-way communication with the experimenters was made possible, so if some emergency occurred, it could become known.

To give a basis of comparison, a matched control group was used which was not subjected to the experimental conditions, but whose members went about their daily routines as usual. The tests consisted of selected items from intelligence tests. Both groups also listened to propaganda material so that its effects could be observed.

The groups were tested prior to the isolation period and afterwards. The deprived group was inferior to the nondeprived (control) group on every test after their period of isolation. The attitudes of the deprived group were changed more by propaganda.

The isolated group reported difficulties of concentration during isolation, with frequent "blank" periods, and mounting confusion in thought processes.

Of the twenty-nine experimental subjects, twenty-five reported hallucinations during the isolation period. Electroencephalographic records showed "that at least some of the mechanisms that are responsible for regulating the electrical activity of the brain are affected . . . and the change seems to persist for some time after the individual has returned to a normal environment."

Generally other experiments treating isolation and sensory deprivation of adults have similar results. "There is the implication of deterioration in at least certain types of cognitive functions such as problem-solving and reasoning. . . . With regard to perceptual findings many subjects show a general disruption which is manifested in deficiencies in visual motor coordination. . . . In general the affective response to sensory deprivation includes boredom, restlessness, irritability, and occasionally anxiety or fear of panic proportions. Descriptions of conditions of subjects after isolation have referred to fatigue, drowsiness, and feelings of being dazed, confused, and disoriented." [5]

You can see that all the evidence points clearly to the need of the human organism for a great wealth of sensory experiences. If the effects are this harmful to adults, how much more if children for long periods of time are deprived.

DR. CHEAVENS: Mrs. Zimmer has made her point very clear and I think it will be further clarified by what Mr. Inman will have to say.

MR. INMAN: I have a very short report on the records of infants born with cataracts which were removed only after the person reached adulthood or near-adulthood.[6] These people showed subnormality of visual perception, although clear vision was possible after the operation. Perception of form was particularly troublesome. Such simple tasks as telling the differences between a rectangle and a triangle were very hard. Recognition of friends by sight was also difficult. Even after eyesight became possible, discrimination by sound and by touch were much keener than by vision. Again, although the physical equipment for visual discrimination was apparently functioning well, there was a heavy penalty because of early deprivation of visual experiences. Of course, it is encouraging that they could learn at all visually, however hard and slow it was.

People born with vision take for granted that anyone of average intelligence and normal apparatus for visual perception will automatically make these discriminations, but such is not the case. There must be ample opportunities for the early use of natural abilities. With most of our innate capacities, unless use is made of them, there will be little or no development.

The social meaning of this line of evidence becomes clear. Wherever in the world there are restricted environments, experience will be restricted. Then development will be retarded and the person will never come close to reaching his capacity.

Most of us are interested in the welfare of our communities. Blighted areas of towns and of larger cities are areas of a poverty of experience for children. The people coming out of these areas are penalized. Add this up and you realize the entire nation is penalized. That a few superior people come from the slums proves nothing. We have no way of knowing how much more superior these people might have been under more favorable circumstances. These existing blighted areas can be done away with. They must be done away with. Intelligent people in communities that are now evolving must never allow such blighted areas to develop. The social heritage of every person in the world should be a comfortable pleasant dwelling, and ample room for living.

Children in such blighted areas are penalized in intellectual ability and the ability to learn, not only because of inferior schools, but because of a complex of factors in the homes and neighborhoods where they live. In most homes and neighborhoods in extremely poor areas, communication between people is limited. The vocabularies of school-age children are meager and inadequate.

DR. CHEAVENS: Mr. Inman's final words are a good introduction to our last topic chosen by Mrs. Putnam.

The Advantage of Reading Aloud

MRS. PUTNAM: I'm sure you'll all understand when I say that for very personal reasons I was most interested in this topic. I am so completely convinced of the benefits of reading to babies that for this first one of mine I may start reading Mother Goose right in the delivery room.

I have enjoyed reading about what Dr. Orvis Irwin of the University of Iowa has done.[7] He interested mothers, whose husbands were laborers, in beginning to read to their children when they were only about a year old. The mothers read a minimum of ten minutes a day. By the time these children were twenty months of age, Dr. Irwin found their language development far superior to the average for families in these neighborhoods.

I was just as interested in the work of Helen Dawe, another teacher, who directed a project which demonstrated how language training affects intelligence.[8] She took eleven orphanage children for special speech and language training. This was done with volunteer helpers only on weekends, with a total of 92 hours over seven and a half months. They had a matched control group for purposes of comparison also from the orphanage, who did not receive the language training.

The training group had an 80.6 I.Q. at the beginning of the training period. The average for the controls was 81.5 I.Q. The children ranged in age from about three and one-half to over six. The training included hearing stories and poems, viewing pictures and talking about them.

At the end of the period, the training children averaged about 95 I.Q., while the control children had dropped to 79 I.Q. This difference of 16 points is very large, and shows the great importance of early educational opportunities. This demonstrates, too, what can be done with volunteer help.

Brain-Development and Stimulating Experiences

DR. CHEAVENS: Some of you may be wondering what the physiological basis is for the benefits of an enriched environment. Let me close the meeting with an account of a long-term project of Dr. David Krech of the University of California at Berkeley. For the past fifteen years, he has carried out a fascinating and important series of experiments.[9] He and his co-workers took a large number of rats and placed them in the most stimulating and interesting environment they could provide. There were mazes to run, ladders to climb, wheels to run in, and all in all, what amounted to a university education for rats. An equal number of rats were kept in relative isolation, away from such a challenging environment.

Almost anybody could predict that the rats in the stimulating environment would turn out to be better performers and faster learners than the deprived rats. This was, of course, the case and is not the result which is of most interest here.

The experimenters enlisted expert physiologists to examine particularly the brains of the two groups of rats. There were marked and very significant differences. The cortexes of the rats from the stimulating environment were much thicker than those of the isolated rats. Blood vessels supplying this "thinking" area of the brain were larger than those of the control rats, meaning, of course, that many of the essentials for thought processes such as oxygen, sugar, and other biochemical necessities were in much more abundant supply than in the control rats.

The investigators also examined the brains of rats that for many generations had been selectively bred according to learning ability,

68   CREATIVE PARENTHOOD

and found approximately the same differences between these rats
and the isolated animals as between the stimulated rats and the
isolated. Which means that Dr. Krech could achieve quickly in one
generation through a stimulating environment what it took many
generations of selective breeding to achieve.

I think we are justified in making inferences for human beings
from these rat experiments. Reasonably we could predict that the
changes in the human brain would probably be much greater under
comparable circumstances than the changes in the rats.

Heredity has long been assigned an important role, and rightly
so, in producing high intelligence in human beings. But it may be
that we can produce the same desirable results through stimulating
environments for all people.

Much of the experimental work with the performance of people
bears out these inferences. We do not know exactly what happens to
the brain of a child when a parent reads to him, talks with him, or
takes him on a walk pointing out objects of interest. We do know
that these and other activities produce good results in the learning
and mental development of the child, and we would be justified in
inferring that there are favorable developmental changes within the
brain.

All of the accumulated evidence points rather clearly to the fact
that, in order to develop to capacity, the human organism needs a
rich and varied experience beginning in infancy and continuing as
long as the person lives.

FOOTNOTES

1. E. J. Gibson and R. D. Walk, "The effect of prolonged exposure
to visually presented patterns on learning to discriminate them." *Journal
of Comparative and Physiological Psychology* 49 (1956), 239–42.

2. A. H. Riesen, "Arrested Vision," *Scientific American* 183 (1950),
16–19.

3. A. H. Riesen, "Plasticity of Behavior," in *Biological and Biochemical Bases of Behavior*, eds. Harlow and Woolsey (Madison,
Wisc.: University of Wisconsin Press, 1958), pp. 424–49.

4. Phillip Solomon, et al., eds., *Sensory Deprivation* (Cambridge,
Mass.: Harvard University Press, 1961), pp. 6–33.

5. Ibid., pp. 228–29.

6. M. V. Von Senden, cited in Fillmore H. Sanford, *Psychology, A Scientific Study of Man* (San Francisco: Wadsworth Publishing Co., 1961), p. 86.

7. Boyd R. McCandless, *Children and Adolescents* (New York: Holt, Rinehart and Winston, 1961), p. 260.

8. Helen C. Dawe, "A study of the effect of an educational program upon language development and related mental functions in young children," *Journal of Experimental Education* 11 (1942), 200–209.

9. David Krech, paper read to the 1966 Southwestern Psychological Association at Arlington, Texas.

8. Advantages to Character Development from Family and Community Life

DR. CHEAVENS: On a very down-to-earth basis, you are probably interested in finding out just what sorts of families produce the "good citizen" and what sorts produce the delinquents. We have some good objective evidence about this. Likewise, you are probably just as interested in what forces outside of the home help to produce these results. When your child enters school, he begins to be exposed more and more to these external influences. His schoolmates will have a great deal to do with his behavior.

Some communities have much lower delinquency rates than others. The community at large will have something to do with your child's behavior. In certain localities it is much more probable that your child will not be delinquent than in other localities. What can be done in your community to increase the probability of constructive behavior for your child?

MRS. DANA: I'm really interested in all of this, primarily since I have the responsibility of six boys. I think I would first like to know what kind of family produces what you call the good citizen.

MRS. WALLACE: Before we answer that one, and I'm very interested in it, too, there is another question we need to answer. Is the rate of delinquency really growing?

MRS. DANA: It seems to me that population growth alone would account for the greater number of crimes.

MR. VICTOR: I can answer that one for you. I've just been looking over the most reliable source of statistics we have—the F.B.I. reports, which are published yearly in booklet form. The frightening fact is that all crimes, and this includes juvenile crime, are increasing at a much greater rate than the population is increasing. This has been true for a number of years. From 1960 to 1968 serious juvenile crimes increased 78 percent, while the number of persons in the age group ten to seventeen increased only 25 percent.[1]

MR. SHELBY: While I value the statistical reports, our personal experiences would also give us the same information. The last time I was in Washington, D.C., my friends living there warned me about crossing downtown parks even in broad daylight. And they warned me to be especially careful at night.

MR. WALLACE: But isn't most of this juvenile crime in the blighted areas of the big cities?

MR. VICTOR: There's a rapidly growing rate of crime in the suburbs, sometimes called "middle-class delinquency" and even in rural areas that formerly had hardly any at all.

MRS. DANA: This is frightening!

MR. SHELBY: I have a neighbor with two teen-age boys, fourteen and sixteen. He says that if he can just keep them out of jail, he'll consider himself as a successful parent.

(There were smiles from the group, but the major reaction seemed to be one of concern.)

MRS. DANA: I'm back to the place of wanting to hear from Dr. Cheavens the kinds of homes that produce the good citizens.

Five Types of Character Development

DR. CHEAVENS: To answer the question of what kinds of families produce the children most prone to poor citizenship and what kinds produce those whose chances are good of becoming good citizens, two behavioral scientists at the University of Chicago, Peck and Havighurst, directed an extensive study of a midwestern town which they fictitiously called Prairie City.[2] They were trying to find out about the character development of the children and youth of this community of 10,000 people. They also tried to find out why character developed as it did.

In a general way among the adults, they found that family, church, and school standards were in agreement. I don't know whether this is true in most communities. And here was an interesting finding: "The community shrugs its shoulders at . . . mild political corruption and is cynical about connections between politics and 'shady' business." [3] Is this true in most communities?

Among the children and young people the investigators studied, they identified five "character types." [4] Let's go from the worst to the best. The first and worst was the "amoral" type. These egocentric youngsters are of a type sometime called the "psychopathic personality." This does not mean they are mentally ill. It means they are morally or ethically ill. They follow whims, wishes, and impulses regardless of the consequences to other people. Their friendships, if such they could be called, are only temporary alliances. They have no internalized moral principles, no conscience or superego, no need for self-control. They are also lacking in foresight, and tend not to see what the results of their behavior will be.

MRS. DANA: Do we have any idea how many people of this kind there are in our country?

DR. CHEAVENS: It is hard to estimate how many people of this kind there are in our country. They really cause a great deal of our trouble as far as illegal behavior is concerned.

What did investigators find out about the families of these potential troublemakers? The families of the "amoral" were "actively rejecting." There was a lack of affection and mutual trust. There was an inconsistency in the behavior of parents described as chaotic. Some parents tended to be very harsh in their punishment; others to be overly lenient and adopting a policy of letting the child do whatever he wished.

The investigators classified a second group as "the expedient." The young people in this group are also self-centered. Their behavior is moral only so long as it suits their purposes and furthers their own interests. Such morality is only a way of gaining a good reputation which will also be an advantage in gaining their ends. They are perfectly willing to engage in dishonest behavior if this will increase their gains, and if they will not be detected. Some of the parents of these children were also too lenient and allowed indiscriminate freedom. Other parents of this group were autocratic and mistrustful. In the first case there was love without consistency, and in the second, consistency without love.

The third classification was described as "irrational-conscientious." This group has a rigid inner code which is not arrived at by rational process. The code is entirely subjective and does not consider consequences to others. The conscience is "blind." Among this type one might find the compulsively law-abiding person, or a criminal who, without thinking, follows the code of his group which he has appropriated second-hand.

The "irrational-conscientious" children come from homes characterized by severe and consistent discipline producing rigid, strong superegos (or consciences), and are loyal to a code delivered to them ready-made.

Another group was the "conforming." These young people had one major principal which was internalized, and this was to conform to the code of the group because they feared disapproval. The true value of the code was not thought through. Hence kindness is not necessarily one of their principles; the code of the group may call for kindness to some, cruelty to others. The rules dictate what is right. The rules are not questioned, even though they may call for destructive as well as constructive behavior.

The "conformers" generally came from autocratic, consistent parents whose punishments were severe, in some cases loving, and in others, not. The children were poured into a rigid mold of unthinking conformity.

The most positive character development, perhaps the only truly positive character development, was found in the group designated "rational-altruistic." Parents were consistent, trustful, democratic, and loving. Punishments were not harsh. The authors write, "to be intelligently and effectively ethical it appears necessary to add to this pattern [of love] the element of democracy, the opportunity to experiment in making decisions, and to develop and trade ideas, unafraid, with parents and other family members."

In summing up, the authors state that "character . . . appears to be predominantly shaped by the intimate, emotionally powerful relationship between child and parents within the family." [5]

Mrs. Sonneman: From what you've been saying, it is easy to conclude that conscience is not the result of direct didactic teaching. Merely telling children how to behave won't do the job. Good behavior patterns seem to develop gradually and by indirection in an atmosphere of confidence and affection in which the children are encouraged to think for themselves, and make many of their decisions. Add to that a maximum of communication between children and parents and you have the broad picture of the family which results in sound character development.

Dr. Cheavens: This careful study of family relationships underlying each of these categories of character I've been talking about may help to show some of the basic causes for many of our serious social problems. We have other studies that tend to support the findings of these researchers. Let me mention only one. Dr. Robert R. Sears and his associates from the Laboratory of Human Development at Harvard studied patterns of child-rearing of more than 300 American mothers. [6] One element of the study dealt with conscience development in the children. The investigators found better conscience development in the children of loving, accepting mothers, and weaker development in the children of rejecting mothers.

The combination of affection and firmness, leading to close identification with parents who are good models, and especially in the sense that their code of behavior is built around consideration for others—these elements are the foundation for the highest ethical development of children.

MRS. ZIMMER: As most of you know, I have the sole responsibility for my two girls. Is there any way I can *be sure* they're going to turn out all right. I suppose I'm looking for some sort of sure-fire guarantee as I face the future.

DR. CHEAVENS: I wish this were possible. About the best we can do is to say that there is a very high probability that a child from the loving, stable family will be nondelinquent and a constructive citizen. And the probability of delinquency of the child coming from a rejecting family, a harsh punitive family, or an overindulgent family, is very high.

MRS. ZIMMER: There are so many of their own age group that can change the picture.

MRS. DANA: My hope is that if their inner development is strong, they'll be able to withstand the destructive forces they meet.

MRS. ZIMMER: You would almost have to make sure that all the families in the community were the right kind before you could have complete confidence.

MRS. WALLACE: I feel Mrs. Dana is right. You do the best you can and then when you turn them loose all you can do is to have faith things will be right.

MRS. ZIMMER: But the community is important. What can communities do to make things better for all the young people?

Community Programs for Reducing Delinquency

DR. CHEAVENS: A very early example is what happened in Vienna under the leadership of one of the pioneers in psychiatry, Alfred Adler, who was a firm believer that altruism could become a way of life for everybody. He felt that most problems, both personal and social, were because people were self-centered. Part of his program of therapy was to "break up the ego-centric goal" of the individual and teach him to be considerate of others and work for the common good. He believed that "Social Interest" was the only goal for mankind and that children could be trained in it until it became as natural to them as "breathing or the upright gait." Adler at one time defined social interest as having the same meaning as "Thou shalt love thy neighbor as thyself." [7]

Here a value had become clear, a value Adler felt all people could achieve. He proceeded to help the teachers of the Vienna schools to catch his vision. Some of them became so effective in demonstrating and teaching social interest that their students were also imbued with the ideal. This account of a great ethical ideal, its exemplifications by many of the teachers of Vienna, and its effect upon their students is one of the most remarkable and encouraging in the annals of contemporary education. You might like to read this story in Phyllis Bottome's biography of Alfred Adler.

One element of encouragement here lies partly in the fact that whatever deficiencies may have existed in the child's earlier personality structure tended to be compensated for to some extent in an enthusiasm for a new way of life which was so rewarding for the students that the effects seemed to have had an enduring quality.

Adler felt that the hope of improving human attitudes and behavior lay in the schools. "The Teacher is the long arm of the family. He can reach the child, at a time when it has passed beyond its parents' control. . . . To teach all the parents in the world how to bring up a child is too ambitious a task for Individual Psychology [Adler's philosophy]. There are too many parents and all are not willing to come to us, but there are not too many teachers; and I have always found teachers ready to find out how to make their own work more successful by learning how to understand the child." [8]

Adler gave frequent demonstrations to teachers from fifty Vienna schools, and from other schools in the surrounding territory. Child guidance clinics were attached to more than thirty schools. Special treatment became available for every school child between the ages of six and fourteen. Every classroom felt the impact of the movement and Gloekel, head of the Vienna schools, instituted weekly group discussions in the classrooms to further the education of students in the ethic of social interest and to improve human relations.[9]

A number of teachers were outstanding in their effectiveness. One of these was Oskar Spiel, a teacher of fourteen-year-old boys. Adler visited the last discussion of the year in Spiel's class. The boys had chosen as their topic "The Meaning of Life." Adler was exhilarated as he heard these students who had formed such close ties with one another and with their teacher. They "had been trained in courage and cooperation; . . . had learned to use social interest instead of egocentricity for the goal of their whole being, until it had become an unconscious happy process, freeing them alike from tension and self-seeking." The ties formed in this class survived into adulthood. At class reunions, nearly all the students came back. Their interest in one another was strong and genuine.[10]

In the thirteen years following the initiation of this program the decrease of delinquency and personality disturbances among youth as recorded by Adolescents' Court of Vienna was remarkable enough to silence the critics of the movement. In order to accomplish this result, Adler had to recruit and train nonmedical personnel. These lay-therapists came largely from the ranks of teachers in the city schools. As teachers revealed aptitude and interest for this work they were given special training.

Typical of these was Ida Lowy, who had been a music teacher prior to her training for the child-guidance clinics. "To watch Ida Lowy conducting a child clinic was to see . . . how human nature can be changed; and what the power is that can change it. . . . Her spirit seemed to penetrate into the core of a child's difficulty with the swiftness of lightning, but unlike lightning, her influence moved with the penetrating gentleness of a completely disinterested love . . . that won an instant response from the child."

So imbued with the ideal of social interest did she become that even when she became the victim of a cruel form of cancer, she continued working in the clinic to within a few weeks of her death. Wracked with pain, she gave no outward sign. "She seemed as it were to surmount the illness itself; and died undemoralized, after the shortest possible period of inaction, her spirit exquisitely cheerful to the last." [11]

What Adler did through the schools of Vienna can be duplicated. The knowledge of bettering human behavior is greater today than it was in Adler's day. Also in his day, reaching all the parents with an educational program might have been a task presenting so many difficulties as to have been impossible. Today, with improved methods of communication, while it is still a mammoth undertaking, it is not impossible. Since it is possible, this goal becomes imperative. That parent education is a large part of bettering the world must be constantly held before us. Human personality can be changed, with the family remaining as the most important and the basic social unit. In other words, we need more groups like this one, willing to give of their time and energy in order to improve relations between parents and children.

MR. WALLACE: I think the story of Adler's influence on Vienna is very inspiring, but he was a man of genius as well as having a big heart. How many cities have anyone like this that can spark off a program for schools and parents?

MRS. WALLACE: I don't believe we can find many like Adler. Since this is true, what can most communities do?

MRS. LOVELACE: If you can find enough interested parents in any community, by working together they can effect a change.

MRS. SONNEMAN: While this is quite an old example, I was reading recently in one of the yearbooks of the National Society for the Study of Education and found an account of what happened in Lisbon, Ohio. The citizens there practically eliminated juvenile delinquency. The leaders in the town at that time became alarmed at the increase in the rates of illegal behavior among the youth. Parents, school personnel, leaders in the churches and other organizations got together and set up a plan for helping children and youth, including a recreational program, a summer camp, and classes to instruct the parents of a number of families. This entire program brought about dramatic improvement and at one period cut delinquent behavior to practically nothing.[12]

From the same source, an example of what a school can do was shown by the old Macy School (now defunct) in Los Angeles. In an area where rates of crime among youth would be expected to run very high, the Macy School conducted such comprehensive programs for parents and children that for many years delinquency was practically nil in that part of the city.[13]

Through cooperative efforts of many people all communities can better themselves. You really don't have to have a genius like Adler.

What the Churches Can Do

MRS. WALLACE: It seems like I'm always talking about what the churches can do. I recently read the story of what took place in El Paso under the leadership of a priest, Father Rahm.[14] South El Paso is a blighted area and was responsible for a great deal of juvenile delinquency. Employing voluntary help from people from many churches of all denominations, Father Rahm succeeded in getting a large number of boys' clubs started in the district, each one setting up an active, positive program for the boys. The rates of delinquency in this area of the city were greatly reduced by this effort through the churches which depended solely on voluntary help.

DR. CHEAVENS: A number of church bodies have demonstrated that the church can be a major factor in the ethical development of the child. The juvenile delinquency rates in these groups is very small indeed. Most of these denominations encourage and foster close ties in the family and in the church. Their congregations tend to be small and their codes of conduct are clear-cut.

One such village, almost homogeneous in its church membership, is Keen, Texas. Most of the children attend the church-sponsored schools rather than public school. The town has no jail and only one law-enforcement officer. His chief function is to protect the town from outsiders. Here the homes, the schools, and the church have done an outstandingly successful job of preventing crime among all age groups.

Several nearby towns of approximately the same population have high rates of illegal behavior. The rate in Keen among the members of the dominant church is practically zero.

In addition to the family atmosphere, and the supplementary work of the schools and the churches, there are other factors that affect delinquency.

Whenever populations are too congested, delinquency rates tend to run high. Almost all the urban renewal projects show that the rate of delinquency goes down if people have better housing and more room.

Recreation programs for youth, including all sorts of activities, clubs, athletics, all kinds of games, and wholesome social life, seem to be effective in reducing delinquency.

Treatment centers for the difficult cases, with enough skilled workers to do preventive work, have demonstrated their effectiveness in reducing delinquency.

From all of the evidence, we can say that juvenile delinquency can be reduced in any community, urban or rural, large or small. It seems that it takes a coordinated effort of many people, and definite plans that attack the problem on all fronts.

FOOTNOTES

1. F.B.I., *Uniform Crime Report* for 1968, p. 1.
2. Robert F. Peck and Robert J. Havighurst, *The Psychology of Character Development* (New York: John Wiley and Sons, 1960).

3. Ibid., pp. 24–25.

4. The discussion of these five types and the homes from which they come is found in ibid., pp. 167–77.

5. Ibid., p. 175.

6. Robert R. Sears, et al., *Patterns of Child-Rearing* (Evanston, Ill.: Row, Peterson, 1957), pp. 362–93.

7. Phyllis Bottome, *Alfred Adler* (New York: Vanguard Press, 1957), pp. 121–22.

8. Ibid., p. 149.

9. Ibid., p. 128.

10. Ibid., pp. 148–53.

11. Ibid., pp. 141–47.

12. Nelson B. Henry, ed., *Forty-Seventh Yearbook of the National Society for the Study of Education*, vol. 1 (Chicago: The University of Chicago Press, 1948), p. 206.

13. Ibid.

14. H. J. Rahm, *Office in the Alley* (Austin, Texas: The Hogg Foundation for Mental Health, 1958).

9. The Advantage of Beginning to Learn at an Early Age

Dr. Cheavens: In an earlier meeting we discussed the advantage to your child in having many rich and varied experiences. As a part of this, there are certain skills that a child can learn at a very early age that seem to be an advantage. What specifically can your child learn at a very early age, and what are the advantages?

All living things seem to have some capacity for learning. This is true even with one-cell animals. As we go higher in the scale, the capacity for learning becomes greater and greater. Between the best of the lower animals (and some of them are very intelligent) and man there is a tremendous gap. We just don't know what the ceiling for human learning is.

Early Beginning of Learning

We know that learning in the human organism begins very early. It has been found that on a very simple scale even the unborn infant can learn. This capacity to learn increases rapidly after birth. You have seen your own children begin to learn from the time they were born. They very quickly learned that they could gain human companionship by crying. Babies learn the cues for feeding time, for baths, and for feelings of comfort and security that come from being held and caressed.

The informal education of the person begins at birth and continues until he dies. The child is learning all the time—some things quickly and easily, others with more difficulty, and more slowly.

He learns attitudes and standards of behavior, what you approve and what you disapprove.

Recently there has been a growing interest in what the very young child should be taught formally by his parents or by other teachers. For example we have discovered that certain skills such as skating and swimming can be taught most children as early as two years of age.

For a very young child to learn to swim, to dive, or to skate doesn't seem to be harmful and may even give the child more self-confidence. Certainly it strengthens the child's body. We must keep in mind that there are great individual variations in children and that what may be desirable for one may not be desirable for another. Children vary considerably in their ability to learn physical skills and also in their motivation for this learning.

MRS. DANA: It seems to me that beginning early would put undue stress on a very young child.

MR. VICTOR: If it becomes a matter of pressure, you are right. But does it have to be put on that basis?

MRS. DANA: How could you keep from it?

MR. WALLACE: Can't you put it on the basis of fun instead of pressure or stress? If the learning is sheer enjoyment that would relieve the child of stress.

MR. VICTOR: You're exactly right. But a great deal of all learning is anything but fun.

For a while I was going every day at noon to a neighborhood swimming pool, because nearly everyone went home for lunch and left the pool uncrowded. But a father and his son, who looked to be about five, started coming to the pool every day. The father was attempting to teach his son to swim. He quarreled with him, criticized every move, ridiculed him until it grew so unpleasant for me to witness that I gave up going to that particular pool.

What was this father teaching his son? To hate the water and the process of learning to swim. And perhaps to hate his father! This is an extreme case, but many a parent causes a child to dislike certain tasks because he expects too much of the child and makes the task ugly by putting on pressure, or by being too critical.

Learning Can Be Fun

MR. WALLACE: All of this acquiring of skills should be kept on a basis of enjoyment. Mainly that's why most of us swim or skate. It's fun! I see no reason why all learning should not be done with enjoyment in mind. When parents begin to put pressure on the child to excel in anything, most children react unfavorably. Why make the process grim and ugly, when it can be enjoyable and beautiful?

DR. CHEAVENS: If you are trying to teach your child anything and find that you are becoming too tense about the child's failure or success, stop for a while and come back to it later when you're not so tense. It's rather hard for some parents to teach their children without becoming irritated by failures. Children sense that irritation and it gives them a feeling of failing not only at the task but as a person in the eyes of their parents. As you can see, this sort of emotional and social experience should be avoided at all costs.

MRS. LOVELACE: Doesn't the child's level of maturation have a lot to do with what he can learn and when he can be taught certain things?

MRS. SHELBY: That makes sense to me. I tried hard to teach each of my three boys to pedal a tricycle beginning at age two. Each one could sit on the trike and push it, but on that coordinated action of pedaling, all three of them were around three years of age before they could get it. Then they got it fast.

Maturity and Readiness to Learn

DR. CHEAVENS: In teaching the very young, we have discovered that while it is advantageous to teach some skills, it is completely pointless to try to teach others. The reason for this is the maturity of the organism. I noticed with a young couple I know quite well that in both toilet training and letting their babies learn to walk they were using the approach that is advocated by the experts. For walking the children were given ample opportunities to pull up and stand, and to walk around holding onto a hand or a finger. But this couple never tried to hurry the process. If they had it would have done no good. When the various systems in the organisms that are required for walking are mature enough, the child will walk if he's had enough opportunities. Even when opportunities seem to be rather limited this is true. In Indian tribes where the mother carries the baby on a board on her back it seems the children walk at about the average age of children who have more physical freedom. Very likely you would still want the child to have the freedom to move and to practice whatever he is able to do.

Parents who keep the baby on a soft mattress where rolling and turning and pushing up are too hard are at least denying the child the fun of trying out his strength. He should be placed on a quilt or a pad on a hard surface where he can twist and turn and roll and push up.

With toilet training this same young couple put no pressure on their children. They gave them opportunities to learn without pressure. And both of the children were toilet trained early enough with this relaxed method.

An experiment was tried with twins on toilet training.[1] The psychologist began with one twin very early and left the other untrained. At about eighteen months, the trained one was barely ahead of the other one. At nineteen months the trained one started improving, but beginning about that time the teaching of the untrained twin began, and in two or three weeks he was as well trained as the one on whom all the time and effort had been spent. At about a year and a half they were mature enough for this special type of learning.

Dr. M. B. McGraw, a psychologist, studied one pair of twins for a number of years, giving Johnny, the inferior twin, special training, while Jimmy, the superior twin, had no special training.[2] This experiment showed that on some skills, such as walking or riding a tricycle, special training presents no advantage at all. Johnny and Jimmy walked and learned to ride the tricycle when they were about equal in age. However, Johnny learned to swim and skate at about sixteen months, and the advantages he gained seemed to establish a superiority which continued to be held. Jimmy learned later and was never as good as Johnny. Also, it seemed that Johnny developed more confidence than Jimmy.

Two other well-known investigators, Gesell and Thompson, used identical twin girls as subjects, twins T and C, as they were called in the report. On stair-climbing and buttoning, the twin with the most practice gained only small, temporary advantages.[3]

These studies were both somewhat limited, but perhaps from them and from other similar studies, some of them involving larger numbers of children, we can glean one important point—not to give a child a learning task for which he is not ready. Discovering when he is ready may sometimes be difficult. But the toilet-training policy of the young couple mentioned above with their two children is certainly a good one. The children were given opportunities to learn without having pressure put on them.

Our studies on toilet training show that most United States

parents attempt to toilet-train their children too early, and also
that rigid, severe toilet training is damaging to the emotional development of the child.

I see no reason why most children should not be given early opportunities to learn to swim, skate, or dance, so long as they are not
pressured to learn. If the child enjoys it and begins to learn, well
and good. If not, nothing has really been lost if it has been kept on
a fun basis.

Mr. Shelby: You mentioned earlier that children can learn
to skate and swim at about two years of age, other things being
equal. What other areas are there in which a very young child
can get an early start? My youngest boy is four and I would like
to give him whatever will be for his good.

Early Learning of Musical Skills

Dr. Cheavens: I don't know how practical this will be for you,
but there are some other areas of learning in which we know most
very young children can make progress. Dr. Arthur Jersild of
Columbia University worked with nursery school children for six
months using forty training periods of about ten minutes each,
teaching pitch and intervals of music.[4] Nineteen children were
trained and twenty-nine similar children were tested but given no
training.

The careful records of equally careful statistical evaluation of
the results showed that the teaching of these three-year-old children
yielded positive results both in learning pitch and intervals of
music. When a retest was made after four months of no training,
the trained children demonstrated a retention of skills both in producing pitch vocally and in the use of intervals.

It might be added that these small children in both groups enjoyed the musical tests, and in the case of those who were trained,
they greatly enjoyed the vocal practice as well. And the experimental children had extended their vocal range with both high and
low notes beyond their original performance. The control children,
of course, did not.

Again, since the children enjoyed the learning process and since
it enhanced their musical ability, I can't see any reason why this
sort of thing should not be done with more very young children.

Mr. Shelby: If enough parents would get together, very likely
they could find a teacher, particularly for the summer.

Early Learning of Arithmetic

Dr. CHEAVENS: One very practical area in which a parent can do it himself is arithmetic. The Castle School of New York City has done pioneering with the very young. Dr. Catherine Stern, research assistant at the New School for Social Research in New York City, and director of the experimental Castle School, has achieved remarkable success in teaching preschool children arithmetic. She says, "When visitors to the Castle School see 3-year-old children playing happily with blocks and cases they can hardly believe that this is the beginning of real arithmetic. It seems so much fun!" [5] With these beginning youngsters there are at first no number names and no counting. There is a counting board with which the child learns to fit blocks into their places according to size, learning to discriminate between large and small. Then there are pattern boards with which the child learns to recognize different amounts according to their distinctive patterns. There is also a unit box with which the child learns to match longer blocks with combinations of smaller ones. This is called the Matching Game and the children love it.

Mr. INMAN: Both of my boys, two and four, are interested in numbers. They learned to count early and I think they would catch on quickly with these games. Where can I get these materials?

Dr. CHEAVENS: Dr. Stern's book is published by Harper & Row in New York. Dr. Stern reports that through sight and touch the child begins by having concrete mathematical experiences. Much of it he discovers for himself. He begins to see and feel and understand relationships between numbers. This is in contrast to the conventional "drill" system and also in contrast to the superficial method in which the child is presumably motivated by solving problems having to do with animals, dolls, and his familiar objects. This is effective as far as it goes, but many teachers using it have not taught underlying principles having to do with arithmetic. Dr. Stern's method teaches the principles through actual experience with designed activities which become games for the children.

There is no inattention or boredom and the child sees his own mistakes. This takes out of the learning situation the unpleasantness of the child's feeling that the teacher disapproves when mistakes are pointed out. This type of mathematical learning transfers to many situations in the child's immediate world. It also constitutes a return of "subject matter" to the classroom. In this regard

Dr. Stern states, "What really matters is the long overdue reconciliation in the classroom of thought and mental discipline with the child's happiness." This type of teaching is totally consistent with the child's "mental health" in a very real sense of the expression.

While many of the children are still very young, they come to the place where the visible and tangible blocks are no longer necessary. The child solves arithmetic problems without them. Now he is beginning to work on a symbolic level. His mind is equipped with the tools of thinking! The child learns to think independently and is capable of solving problems on his own.

"The child's entire attitude toward arithmetic is changed. The joy of discovery and the feeling of achievement accompany his work. When presented with our materials, he does not need extrinsic motivation to learn arithmetic. He loves to experiment with the blocks, he is captivated by the intriguing behavior of numbers, and he is eager to explore this field—as far as we will permit him to go." [6]

MR. SHELBY: This sounds great. I think I'll give it a try with my four-year-old Carl.

MR. INMAN: We hear a lot about teaching preschool children to read. Would you mind discussing this and giving us some guidelines?

MRS. SONNEMAN: I can give a personal report. I didn't hear of the Doman method in time to teach my second grader. But my five-year-old girl loves to read and my chief trouble is finding enough of the large print books to keep her satisfied.

Early Learning of Reading

DR. CHEAVENS: The feasibility of teaching reading to the very young was highly publicized through an article in the *Ladies Home Journal* written by a team of dynamic people.[7] These men have succeeded, even beyond the expectations of most of the experts, in two achievements. The first was teaching children from an unbelievable ten months of age to five years of age how to read. The second was that they have taught parents to teach their very young children to read.

This team of experts have found that the best time for learning to read is when the child reaches the tender age of two!

The first principle used is that this must be entirely a happy experience for the child! It will be if it is done right, and the authors insist and have demonstrated that most parents can be successful. They also insist that the learning periods be short, only a few seconds to begin with.

The principle of familiarity is also used, using first body-image words, and then words denoting objects with which the child is familiar.

The first step is teaching the child to discriminate between letters six inches high. The next step is teaching the body-image vocabulary, and next the "environmental vocabulary." The child finally reads from a book, a triumphant beginning of the marvelous adventure of reading! Since the *Journal* is available in almost every library and lists sources from which materials may be ordered, there is no reason why interested parents (and what parents wouldn't be interested) cannot purchase the materials and familiarize themselves with the process. Doman now has a book published entitled *How to Teach Your Baby to Read*.[8]

The public schools in Denver are distributing a manual to help parents instruct their preschool children. They report thousands of preschool children learning to read.[9]

One of the most fascinating experiments in the instruction of the very young is being directed by a Yale sociologist, Dr. Omar K. Moore, who has worked on an experimental project at the Hamden Hall Country Day School near New Haven, Connecticut.[10] Children spend one half hour a day with a "talking typewriter." They learn to type with the touch system and to read at the same time. The child makes progress by satisfying his curiosity. He explores and as he explores, he learns. And the children are entranced by the process!

But what do we know about the outcome of early learning such as this? While there is much here that yet needs exploring and careful study, most of the evidence seems to point to the advantages of early learning.

MR. VICTOR: I have read a few articles that were very critical of teaching children to read at these early ages. But I haven't gone into this thoroughly. Do you have any evidence that would shed light on the question?

DR. CHEAVENS: On the negative side, one of the earlier studies that a good many educators are still citing as evidence that early entrance to school is damaging to a child was made in the schools of Oak Ridge, Tennessee.[11] It involved 103 children who had entered school before they were six years old. This study showed these

children in the sixth grade not up to grade level in achievement nor
as well adjusted socially as children who entered school when they
were a year older. But why?

The investigator explains it on the basis of age differences, but
she is also fair in admitting that, "inevitably, the younger school
entrants are frequently presented with situations that are beyond
their development abilities, and as a result they are not able to
realize their maximum achievement capacity and are likely to
develop personality problems."

It seems that the educational system was at fault by putting
pressures on these younger children. There is no reliable case
made out in this study that age was to blame. With any age
group, if you subject children to pressures beyond their capacities,
you are going to retard achievement and cause personality disturbances.

In addition to what has already been said in favor of preschool
reading, in a Denver experiment involving more than 10,000 four-
and five-year-old children, Dr. Arthur R. Olson, Director of
Denver's Elementary Education, reported that "children in the
original group did consistently better than those who did not
participate." [12]

The NEA *Journal* carried a debate on this subject in the November 1963 issue.[13] The supporting evidence pointing to the
advantages of early reading is, in my opinion, greater than the
evidence pointing in the other direction. Naturally, there are a
good many issues here that are unsettled. We need many carefully designed experiments to help determine what is best for the
child.

Dr. Dolores Durkin, the author of part of the above article and
then at Teacher's College of Columbia University, followed the
studies on preschool learning for a number of years. She summed
up the evidence on a California study and one made in New York
in the *Elementary School Journal*.[14] Concerning the results of the
programs she wrote that none of the earlier readers developed
reading problems when they started to school. For some children,
an early start seemed distinctly advantageous. This was true of
low I.Q. students as well as the superior. These last, after five
years, had reading achievement that was significantly higher than
that of superior I.Q. students who did not learn to read early.

As things stand now, if a parent began a gradual program of
teaching reading and arithmetic to very young children, using
some of the tested systems and making sure that periods of in-

struction were relaxed and very brief, I can see nothing but advantages accruing to most children.

Our very young children are learning something all the time, anyway. Some of them stay glued to television, watching in the main inferior to mediocre programs, and some of them definitely harmful, for hours every day. Why not spend some time teaching the young child something useful and constructive which at the same time will be fun?

Since the group discussions ended, Dr. Durkin has published two informative books on the subject of early reading.[15] She does not ever take the position that all children should be taught reading at an early age, but that the individual child must be considered.

However, as one reads these books, once again there seems to emerge an inescapable conclusion. For most children, with good instruction, the early learning of reading has produced no undesirable results, but rather brought many advantages.

Further important evidence has also been published since these group discussions about the education of very young children.

This comes from a University of Wisconsin experimental study made in Milwaukee with infants from the most blighted area.[11] The project has been going on for four and a half years. Children of both the experiment and matched "control" groups came from a "classic urban slum," which showed a much higher rate of mental retardation among school children than any other area of the city. The I.Q.'s of the forty mothers of the experiment children were measured and found to be under 70.

The investigators discovered that apparently social environment rather than genetic factors accounted for the high rate of mental retardation. One of the challenges of the study was to see if "intellectual deficiency might be prevented." The major social factor contributing to the disadvantage of the environment was the close association of the retarded mothers to their developing infants.

The educational program with both mothers and infants started right after the baby was born with visits in the homes of the experimental children for several hours a day. Some weeks later both mother and infant began going to the Infant Education Center. The infants were exposed to "every aspect of sensory language stimulation." The mothers were given classes in homemaking and baby-care.

The I.Q.'s of the children of the experimental group rose over 50 percent in four years, with the highest reaching 135. The children who were given the developmental opportunities averaged 33 I.Q. points higher than the control children who had received no special training. The experimental children are averaging higher I.Q.'s than their age group for the entire country.

All along many people have felt that the head-start program began with children too late. The investigators of Heber's Infant Education Center have concluded that this is the case, and that what is needed, if the disadvantaged are to develop, is to start with them as infants.

When the experimental children were from nineteen to twenty-five months of age, their vocabularies began to expand rapidly. In the "control" group many of the children could not yet talk at twenty-eight months, and vocabulary production began at that late date in a very limited way.

This well-designed and well-carried out project shows clearly that we can help the disadvantaged to develop into constructive citizens if we will. Now we are faced with the question: "Will we?"

Of course the evidence here demonstrates that our very young children can profit by broad exposure to cultural enrichment, including constructive language and other sensory experiences.

FOOTNOTES

1. Myrtle B. McGraw, "Neural maturation as exemplified in achievement of bladder control," *Journal of Pediatrics* 16 (1940) 580–90.

2. Myrtle B. McGraw, *Growth: A Study of Johnny and Jimmy* (New York: Appleton Century Company, 1935); idem, "Later Development of Children Specially Trained During Infancy: Jimmy and Johnny at School Age," *Child Development* 10 (1939), 1–19.

3. A. Gesell and Helen Thompson, "Twins T and C from infancy to adolescence," *Genetic Psychological Monographs* 24 (1941), 3–121.

4. Arthur T. Jersild, "The Effects of Early Musical Training," in *Readings in Child Psychology*, ed. Wayne Dennis (Englewood Cliffs, N.J.: Prentice-Hall, Inc., 1963), pp. 369–78.

5. Catherine Stern, *Children Discover Arithmetic* (New York: Harper & Bros., 1949), p. 27.

6. Ibid., p. 289.

7. Glenn Doman, George L. Stevens, Reginald C. Orem, "You Can Teach Your Baby to Read," *Ladies Home Journal* (May 1963), pp. 58–64.

8. Glenn Doman, *How to Teach Your Baby to Read* (New York: Random House, 1964).

9. "Two-year-old Readers?" *Newsweek* 60 (July 9, 1962), 46–47.

10. Maya Pines, "How Three-year-olds Teach Themselves to Read and Love it," *Harper's*, May 1963, pp. 58–64.

11. Inez B. King, "Effect of Age of Entrance into Grade I Upon Achievement in Elementary School," *Elementary School Journal*, February 1955, pp. 331–36.

12. "Two-year-old Readers?" op. cit.

13. Dolores Durkin and W. D. Sheldon, "Should the very young be taught to read?" *NEA Journal*, November 1963, pp. 20–24.

14. Dolores Durkin, "After Five Years," *Elementary School Journal* 64 (Dec. 1963), 143–48.

15. Dolores Durkin, *Children Who Read Early* (New York: Teachers College Press, 1966); *Teaching Them to Read* (Boston: Allyn and Bacon, 1970).

16. Stephen P. Strickland, "Can Slum Children Learn?" *American Education*, July 1971.

10. Advantages and Disadvantages from Movies, Comic Books, and Television

DR. CHEAVENS: From talking with most of you previously, I know the deep concern you have over the general effect of the mass media upon your children. You do not want to forbid them to watch appropriate programs, but your chief concern has to do with what is harmful and what is constructive.

What evidence do we have of mass media's effect upon your child? As far as opinion goes, there is considerable conflict. But opinion is notoriously unreliable. On some angles of this question for a number of years I tended to quote the opinion of the experts. Some of those opinions are now being demonstrated as wrong by reliable, objective studies.

Studies on the Effects of Movies

The objective evidence on moving pictures goes pretty far back. One of the best early books was published in 1933, showing how movies affected the social attitudes of school children.[1] The essence of the report in the book was that movies had a decided influence on social attitudes. A highly emotional racist movie caused the viewers to become more race-prejudiced. On the other hand, a picture demonstrating tolerance produced more tolerance in the viewers. This study was done by two University of Chicago psychologists and was a well-received, objective piece of work. The investigation made follow-up studies showing that the changes in attitude persisted for months after the picture was seen.

Perhaps these results are about what most observant people

know, anyway. Your children learn best through the avenues of vision and hearing. With the addition of color and depth, the picture becomes more lifelike and more effective. Children identify with the characters in the drama, feeling with them, thinking with them, and making choices with them.

Even brief exposures such as used by advertisers are effective in producing certain types of behavior among great masses of viewers, and the constant aim of the advertisers is to influence more and more people to buy the product. One tobacco company has recently reported a considerable boost in the sales of its product due to a line of brief ads appealing to hostility in human nature. And actually, their line of advertising is so ridiculous that anyone influenced by it must be terribly immature. Of course your children are immature. The average American television program is supposed to appeal to people who have not gone beyond the twelfth year in emotional and mental maturity.

You, and many other parents today, are raising serious questions about the effects of children's viewing so much violence on television. The same thing is true of the movie theater, but most children are not exposed to as many theater-shown motion pictures as they are T.V. programs. The total hourly exposure of most of your children to T.V. programs is very large.

Fortunately, we have some well-designed, controlled experiments that show what exposure to programs of violence does to the behavior of children.[2] In reporting his experiments, Dr. Albert Bandura, Stanford University psychologist, first states that the rapid increase of television "aggression and violence," which some investigators brand as brutality, attracts and holds larger audiences than nonviolent programs. He also comments on the uncritical acceptance of glib opinions that T.V. brutality has little or no effect upon children. "Precise information," he states, "can come only through carefully controlled laboratory tests in which the children themselves participate." For this reason a series of such experiments was conducted at the psychological laboratories at Stanford University.

The experiments tested "the extent to which children will copy aggressive patterns of behavior" as shown by adult models in real life, or on film, or in cartoons. One group of children saw no aggressive models. This group served as a control group for purposes of comparison.

The children of the experiment "were not too inclined to give precise imitations of the cartoon character." But both observing the "real life" adult aggression and adult aggression "on film" lowered the child's inhibitions against acting "in a violent, aggresive manner." The experimental child showed almost twice as much aggressiveness in the observation room as the control children who had not seen the adult models of aggression. Film violence stimulated the experimental children to greatly increased hostile behavior, but their observation of real life and film adult violence tended "to shape the *form* of the child's aggressive behavior."

Another element of the experiment investigated the effects of "punishing the bad guy." The stereotyped opinion is that what the child learns from observing antisocial models will be offset if in the end right triumphs, the "good guy" is rewarded, and the "bad guy" is punished.

In the experiments, if antisocial behavior paid off, the children were all too ready to imitate it. The children who saw aggressive behavior punished showed "very little imitative aggression." Even the children who imitated the bad guy were highly critical of this behavior. They imitated him, in spite of their disapproval of his behavior, because his behavior paid off.

Dr. Bandura points out that this last experiment involved only one incident of punished or rewarded behavior and that most films show a long series of aggressive acts many of which appear to pay off, with the villain only briefly punished in the end. This punishment may have weak effects upon the child, with the repeated earlier rewards to the villain having a greater effect.

In another series which studied the effects of punished versus rewarded aggression, children were more imitative of rewarded aggression. But when the children were offered attractive rewards if they would imitate the violent model's behavior, inhibitions quickly disappeared, and the very close imitation of the model's aggression showed that the children had learned well the lesson of how to behave aggressively.

Another investigator delved into the effects of films of violence on adolescents and adults. Dr. Walters of the University of Toronto discovered that adults and adolescents behaved much more aggressively after viewing the switchblade knife scene in *Rebel Without a Cause*, as compared with the control group which viewed an instructional film.

MR. VICTOR: The following incident happened to the nine-year-old son of one of my friends and certainly is in line with the research you mentioned. This boy was then in the habit of just going to his room at bedtime, cutting off the light, and going to sleep immediately.

His parents allowed him to go alone to the theater to see an afternoon film involving Frankenstein and Abbott and Costello, thinking it was only a comedy and would therefore have no ill effects upon the boy. The film was evidently more a horror movie than a comedy. That night the boy could not go to sleep. He kept seeing horror images of Frankenstein. It was almost two months before his sleeping habits were restored to normal.

I don't mean I can prove anything, of course, by citing one case. Seeing this film was a terrific emotional upset to this boy. Other children may have seen it without being so disturbed. However, there are a good many who have bad reactions. There are cases of adults, too, who suffer serious emotional trauma from seeing horror movies. Part of this is a matter of individual temperament. Some children are much more insensitive than others. But sometimes we may think our child is insensitive when he is not.

Effects of Comic Books

Mrs. WALLACE: Some of my friends have been upset over the effect of comic books on their children. Neighbors of mine had an interesting experience when their son was about seven years old. He complained to his parents that he could not go to sleep. When they questioned him he told them that the faces of the people in the horror comics he had been reading kept coming before him. These horror comics had been given him by a friend without the parents' knowing about it.

The parents started letting the boy choose his own books. They wisely let the boy ban the books that were frightening him. He did a good job of this, and all the horror books were eliminated by the boy himself.

This same couple also decided to institute an incentive program for constructive reading. For every good book their son read, they would reward him by letting him go to the bookstore and select for himself another good book. This improved his reading and also gave him the beginning of a large fund of information, since most of the books he read were factual.

Another strategy they used successfully was to have the boy read a page or two aloud and then either the father or the mother do the same. This was particularly effective with an otherwise good book which started off slowly or was relatively difficult. Usually as they read farther into the book the boy would work up enough interest to read it for himself. If the parents did not finish the book, they would ask their son to tell them about the part they missed.

DR. CHEAVENS: Many children have been motivated to read through comic books, and there are some very fine ones available, such as the Classic Comics. Then there are others that are merely harmless and fun to read.

Effects of Watching Television

Some parents will themselves choose the T.V. program of violence and brutality because of their own interest, and will carelessly allow the child to sit up late and see it through. Television and movies can be wonderfully entertaining and instructive. But surely parents should be more selective in the programs and movies they allow children to see.

From all the evidence, it would seem that parents are extremely short-sighted in their policies relating to all the mass media to which their children are constantly exposed. It is the opinion of a large number of people dealing with children that our American children are greatly overstimulated emotionally, particularly from movies or television programs calculated to produce feelings of fear or hostility or a combination of them.

MRS. WALLACE: I remember reading one authority who said that American children were not only overstimulated emotionally but underexpressed. They watch too much and participate too little. We encouraged our own children to play outdoors as much as possible and take part in group games.

DR. CHEAVENS: I think you have a very positive program when you do that. I also agree with the statement that our children are underexpressed. Instead of teaching children methods of aggression, we could as easily teach them how to direct and control aggression and fear in positive ways. Outspoken parental sentiment, especially letters protesting T.V. and movie violence and praising films showing children how to deal effectively with their destructive emotions, will have to become widespread before changes occur. Whenever constructive films are shown, it always helps to write in and ask for more of the same. T.V. producers are very sensitive to letters of both approval and disapproval. The use of political control is the most important, however.

The effect of T.V. advertising upon children and adolescents is considered by the Independent Television Authority, controlling T.V. advertising in England, to be so powerful that ads "that overemphasize the pleasure of smoking, appeal to manliness, feature youth's heroes, present romantic situations or give the impres-

sion that smoking is an essential part of life" are definitely pro-
hibited.[3] British cigarette companies have agreed not to advertise
on T.V. before 9 P.M. to avoid influencing the very young. Italy
has become rational enough to ban all cigarette advertising.

In the United States the American Public Health Association
makes the prediction that, based on the present death rate from
lung cancer, of children now in school a million will die of lung
cancer before they reach the age of 70.

The tobacco companies have at last taken their commercials off
of television. This was due to the legal ban against such advertising. They were compelled to discontinue their public relations program.

One cheering word in this sad, sordid story came from one small
T.V. station in Concord, California, where on a purely voluntary
basis cigarette commercials were banned as the result of the Sur-
geon General's report on cigarette-smoking and health. Victor Ives,
Vice President of KWUN said, "I don't see how broadcasting
cigarette advertising can be consistent with the public interest in
view of the government report." Ives went on to say that television
should not be "all take and no give," and that his station would
broadcast 30-second spot announcements discouraging smoking.[4]
It goes without saying that this small station lost money by its policy. But it is to be greatly admired.

The Problem of Advertising

The cynical advertising campaign of cigarettes in newspapers
and in magazines continues under the banner of "free enterprise"
in the U.S. Psychologist Dr. Carl Rogers, writing about the possi-
bility of controls of human behavior through psychological methods, says, "We can choose to use our growing knowledge to enslave
people in ways never dreamed of before, depersonalizing them, controlling them by means so carefully selected that they will perhaps
never be aware of their loss of personhood."[5]

Among the young people of the United States this has already
happened in certain areas of their living. What is responsible for
it is not some threatening foreign power (if this were so, we would
be appalled and openly hostile). What is responsible for this seduc-
tion of the minds and bodies of the young is the most important of
the gods in our pantheon—Big Money. Large corporations, through
the use of conditioning processes in mass media, are becoming almost the equivalent of Orwell's Big Brother prophesied in his book,

1984. This exploitation of the minds and emotions of the very young is the proud achievement of many large industries and businesses.

MRS. ZIMMER: Not too long ago a young mother I know was telling about her troubles with her four-year-old son. He has become rigidly conditioned through T.V. programs to eating only one brand of breakfast cereal, which the mother considers to be inferior. The mother finally won on the use of a better brand, but only after several major emotional crises with the youngster. And now she is applying her own brand of censorship to the offending program. I have had some problems like this with my two.

MRS. VICTOR: If you censored all offending programs, how many would be left? Probably very few. The objective of most advertisers seems to be to hook the most consumers, no matter what the advertising or the product does to the consumer or to the truth, regardless of ethics, with no consideration for the future of our youth. Unless these irresponsible advertisers can develop some sense of responsibility for the welfare of our country, our youth will continue to be exploited for the sake of declaring larger dividends. This is the most insidious form of manipulation when those being exploited are not even aware that it is going on.

DR. CHEAVENS: A leading authority on advertising, Thomas P. Coffey, now projects editor for the World Publishing Company, commenting on this insidious process by advertisers, has said, "Not content merely to ogle, stimulate, inveigle the public, from without, into purchases, an ad man is now concerned with controlling, from within, the entire process of human thinking in respect to the desire for commodities and the actual decision to pay for them." [6]

Advertisers are now concerned with probing the secrets of the unconscious and using man's deeply submerged processes to capture him without his being aware of what is happening. The consumer is no longer his own man, but has been enslaved by the philosophy of constantly consuming more and more (while enjoying his possessions less and less). The aim of advertising is to create an avid, object-hungry consumer, beginning in early childhood and continuing until the moment of death. During this brief span, man must never be content with what he has. He must be perennially dissatisfied with all his possessions. He must have more and more gadgets, and more and more equipment to take care of his more and more gadgets. He must throw away his gadgets as obsolete as soon as a slightly altered model appears.

The American Association of Advertising Agencies has recently come out with a new code.[7] In this new code, which is admirable as far as it goes, the organization forswears false or misleading statements and suggestions, or anything which may be "offensive to public decency." Nothing is said, however, about the devious and sinister methods of distorting emotional and mental processes in order to sell merchandise. As dangerous as are the false advertisements, this bid by big business through advertising for mind control of the American public is the real problem; it constitutes one of the greatest threats to our society.

Vance Packard, widely read author on psychological methods in advertising, in a speech to the advertising conference tells of the deep motivation in a husband or father buying more insurance: "They see that they are moving from the role of being protected to being a protector. They see it very often as a symbol of their own sexual virility. So the more money they lay on the line for insurance, the more potent they feel. The Institute [for Motivational Research] said, 'Life insurance can become a reassuring symbol of masculine power and sexuality.' "[8]

Aldous Huxley, writing about the exploitation of the very young by advertising, quotes an advertising specialist as stating: "Think of what it can mean to your firm in profits if you can condition a million or ten million children, who will grow up into adults trained to buy your product, as soldiers are trained to advance when they hear the trigger words, 'Forward March!' "[9]

Richard L. Tobin, communications editor of the *Saturday Review*, writing about the lack of ethical practices in advertising, states "The American public will tolerate a very great deal before it explodes, but when it does explode, the offender beware." [10] The time has come for intelligent American parents to become aware of the mind-molding processes of commercial advertising and to explode.

The word of David Ogilvy carries weight in the advertising world. He runs a 55-million-dollar-a-year agency. This expert advocates "informative factual advertising," which, from experience, he says is actually more effective in "sales results" than "combative" or "persuasive" advertising. He further states that "if all advertisers would give up flatulent puffery, and turn to . . . factual, informative advertising . . . , they would not only increase their sales, but they would place themselves on the side of the angels. The more informative your advertising, the more persuasive it will be." [11] Mr. Ogilvy has demonstrated this again and again.

He cites a poll [12] conducted among leaders in many institutions answering the question, "Should advertisers give the facts and only the facts?" The results of the poll in terms of percentage of those answering yes were:

Religious leaders	76 percent
Editors of highbrow publications	74 percent
High school administrators	74 percent
Economists	73 percent
Sociologists	62 percent
Government officials	45 percent
Deans of colleges	33 percent
Business leaders	23 percent

This poll points up the amazing fact that a high percentage of important leaders, government officials, college deans, and business leaders seem not to want the public to know the facts about what is advertised.

Commenting on television advertising, he says, "It is television advertising which has made Madison Avenue the arch-symbol of tasteless materialism . . . . I have a vested interest in Madison Avenue, and I doubt whether it can survive without drastic reform. . . .

"Hill and Knowlton report that the vast majority of thought-leaders now believe that advertising promotes values that are too materialistic. The danger to my bread-and-butter arises out of the fact that what the thought-leaders think today, the majority of voters are likely to think tomorrow. No, . . . advertising should not be abolished. But it must be reformed." [13]

Just as the mass media have been employed for destructive purposes, they have amply demonstrated their effectiveness to influence human behavior positively. One example is the medical profession's success in gaining the cooperation of very high percentages of vast metropolitan populations in the immunization procedure with the Sabin oral vaccine against polio. In bringing about such widespread action there first had to exist in the minds of parents a feeling of real need for this immunization. When a need of this kind exists, the united action of newspaper, radio, and T.V. can achieve very positive results.

What can we do? We can write letters approving constructive T.V. programs and advertising, and criticizing that which we think is undesirable. (Of course the amount of this sort of thing one person can do is limited.) We can also work to get various organizations to exert their influence. Public opinion is a powerful thing.

In the meantime, every home can begin to be more selective about what the children watch. A very small amount of T.V. viewing goes a long way. Many children sit for hours when they should be out playing or doing something in which they are more active than in passive T.V. viewing. We can help our children learn to express themselves creatively—which is the subject we will discuss next.

FOOTNOTES

1. R. C. Peterson and L. L. Thurstone, *Motion Pictures and the Social Attitudes of Children* (New York: The Macmillan Co., 1933), pp. 1–38.

2. Albert Bandura, et al., "Identification as a Process of Individual Learning," *The Journal of Abnormal and Social Psychology* 63, no. 2 (1961), 311–18; idem, "Transmission of Aggression Through Limitation of Aggressive Models," *The Journal of Abnormal and Social Psychology* 63, no. 3 (1961), 575–82; or see the popular article in *Look*, Oct. 22, 1963, pp. 46–52.

3. *The Kiplinger Magazine*, December 1962.

4. "KWUN's Refusal of Cigarette Commercials," *Saturday Review* 47 (Feb. 8, 1964), 24.

5. Carl R. Rogers and B. F. Skinner, "Some Issues Concerning the Control of Human Behavior: A Symposium," *Science* 127: 1057–1066.

6. Thomas P. Coffey, "Advertising Techniques and the Moral Law," in *Advertising in America*, ed. Payntz Tyler (New York: The H. W. Wilson Company, 1959), pp. 169–76.

7. R. L. Tobin, "Code of Ethics for Advertising," *Saturday Review* 45 (June 9, 1962), 47–48.

8. Vance Packard, "The Hidden 'Why's' of our Behavior," in *Advertising and the Subconscious*, ed. Edmund Wooding (Ann Arbor: Bureau of Business Research, Univ. of Michigan, 1958), p. 41.

9. Aldous Huxley, *Brave New World Revisited* (New York: Harper & Row, 1958), p. 53.

10. Tobin, op. cit.

11. David Ogilvy, *Confessions of an Advertising Man* (New York: Atheneum Press, 1963), p. 151.

12. Ibid., pp. 151–52.

13. Ibid., pp. 163–64.

11. Advantages of Creative Development

DR. CHEAVENS: It is doubtful if one period will be enough for the topic of creativity, so we will continue the discussion in the next session.

It has been a joy to watch how a young couple near our home have given their children opportunities for creative activities. They have gone beyond that and recognized their creative efforts and approved them. With this encouragement the daughter is continually improving her drawing ability, and the son has made an airplane that is really superior work for a three-year-old.

MRS. WALLACE: I wish at first we could get a definition of creativity. People have so many different activities. How many of them can be called creative?

DR. CHEAVENS: Of course we are glad when people get into constructive activities, but you are right that not all of these are creative.

If you define creativity broadly, then many of these activities would be included. Perhaps as our discussion goes on each of us will be able to evolve his own working definition of it.

Everybody Has Creative Possibilities

We are beginning to find out a great deal about creativity. There has been more research on it in the last dozen years than in perhaps the fifty years before that. It seems that everybody of average intelligence has creative potential. Even some considerably below average have it. You may then feel encouraged about your children having some creative capacity that can be developed.

Irving Taylor, a social psychologist, helps in defining creativity by classifying different levels of the process. In this way he gives a broad definition that helps to answer Mrs. Wallace's question. One of these he calls "expressive creativity" in which "skills, originality, and the quality of the product are unimportant." Spontaneity and freedom are the basis for this level of creativity. "The more spontaneous and independent children are allowed to be, the more creative they may become later on." [1] No living person who has a means of self-expression need be denied this type of creativity.

When I was working with mentally retarded children I saw many examples of their expressive creativity in drawing and painting and interpretive dancing. It's encouraging for parents to know that every child can find some way of expressing this almost magic potential for creative activity!

Dr. Taylor goes on to classify the higher levels of creativity in which the quality of the product becomes more important. Productive creativity, says Dr. Taylor, is the result of skills to gain mastery over some part of the environment. "Inventive creativity" is ingenuity in seeing new and unusual relationships between previously separated parts. "Innovative creativity" involves having such a clear understanding of the basic principles that improvements are made through making changes.

What he calls "emergentive creativity" is the discovery of a new principle or assumption. The work of Freud and of Einstein, of Picasso and Frank Lloyd Wright are in this category, which Dr. Taylor calls "the highest form of creative power."

Of course, to reach these higher and more useful forms of creativity the person has to go through the exploratory periods of expressive creativity, finding out what he can do, and what he likes to do, by freely trying out all sorts of activities.

I observed a young father tooling leather. His three-year-old daughter was watching. After she had carefully observed the process, she sat down with the leather-working tools and pounded out a truly beautiful design on a small piece of leather. Her father was not afraid to let her use the tools and didn't discourage her because she was too small. This is a good example of how creativity starts.

Qualities of Creative People

Most parents would enjoy a book by the late Dr. Abraham Maslow of Brandeis University, *Toward a Psychology of Being*. In it he tells of a study he made of forty-five creative people. [2]

These people were not necessarily geniuses. They had "that more widespread creativeness which is the universal heritage of every human being that is born, and which seems to co-vary with psychological health." Maslow first had to free his own mind of some conventional ideas about creativity as he made his study. One of these was thinking that creativity was only in artistic activities, such as painting, composing music, or writing poetry. Unconsciously he had assumed that "creativeness was the prerogative solely of certain professions." He learned that "a first-rate soup is more creative than a second-rate painting, and that, generally, cooking or parenthood or making a home could be creative while poetry need not be . . . ."

A conversation that is fresh and spontaneous can be creative. A laboratory experiment certainly may be. A simple invention involving insight into a human need would be included. The constructive expression of emotion might be classified as creative. Anything fresh, original, inventive, spontaneous, useful, an idea bringing pleasure to people, a helpful attitude—all and any of these are within the scope of Dr. Maslow's concept.

Dr. Maslow found that his self-actualizing people were "more spontaneous and expressive than average people. They were more natural and less inhibited in their behavior, which seemed to flow out more easily and freely with less blocking and self-criticism." In many ways they were more innocently childlike.

These creative people were "relatively unfrightened by the unknown, the mysterious, the puzzling, and often were positively attracted by it . . . ."

The author gives as the main reason for the creativeness of these unusual individuals he studied their relative freedom from fear. They were not afraid of what other people thought or would say. Having less neurotic need of others, they could act more independently but also with less hostility. "They were more self-accepting than average."

Here we have a striking and comprehensive picture of the creative personality according to the definition of one who has made a deep and careful study of many creative people.

You doubtless have a genuine concern about the development of your children in the area of religion. When you read Dr. Maslow's book, you will notice that practically all of his self-actualizing people had what he calls "self-transcending" experiences, which really correspond to what most of us call positive religious experience. These experiences also seem to stimulate creativity.

Steps in the Creative Process

You and many other parents like you would appreciate information on the steps in the creative process. If you know these and can recognize them, you can see when the creative process is at work in your children, and give it time as well as a friendly atmosphere in which to develop and continue to grow until the final creative product is achieved.

Graham Wallas of London University was an early authority on the subject whose keen perception, after much study, has given us the steps.[3] He calls them Preparation, Incubation, Illumination, and Verification. These steps, he says, apply to originating a new principle or an invention, or the poetical expression of a new idea. He says also, "Yet, even when success in thought means the creation of something felt to be beautiful and true, rather than the solution of a prescribed problem, the four states of . . . Preparation, Incubation, Illumination, and Verification of the final result can generally be distinguished from each other."

Anything creative is connected with earlier events in the person's experience. These may be emotions, physical events, reading, conversations, observations, sensations, or any of a host of experiences. This Wallas calls "Preparation." Preparation may be conscious or unconscious, casual or controlled.

The period of incubation is the time when the person may not be consciously considering his idea or problem. He may be walking or merely resting. He may be reading in a relaxed fashion. Or he may be engaged in any of a number of activities not relevant to his creation. Incubation takes time. In many of our educational systems, a teacher becomes alarmed if a student is not busy. Yet if we expect true creativity we must give time for the period of incubation. Somtimes this may be branded as idleness, but even idleness may be productive.

One educational psychologist, Edith Weisskopf, in commenting on the factor of ample time free from pressure as a necessity for creative work, writes, "Most educators in their . . . admonitions . . . stress the importance of industry. Yet, if we scan through the literature on creativity, we find statements such as the following: 'Though without industry great intellectual work cannot be done, yet mere industry may prevent creation.' "[4] The constant activity enforced by many educators does not give young people the leisure which is an essential prerequisite for intellectual or artistic creation. ". . . the question remains unanswered, why, among the four states of the creative process, namely, preparation, incubation, illumination and verification, we prepare children for the first and last stage only, and completely ignore the other stages." [5]

The period of illumination is the time when the new idea comes —for a painting, a story, an article, an invention, or the solution to any kind of problem. Wallas, who had investigated the creative process at work in many outstanding people, tells of the great German physicist Helmholtz, who said that after his investigation (preparation) "in all directions . . . happy ideas come unexpectedly without effort, like inspiration. So far as I am concerned, they have never come to me when my mind was fatigued, or when I was at my working table. . . . They came particularly readily during the slow ascent of wooded hills on a sunny day." Illumination is when the new idea or ideas come consciously to the mind after the period of relaxing incubation, during which the thoughts are free and perhaps wandering, but in any case, at ease.

The step of verification comes when the creative work is done, when the painting is completed as a work of art, or the problem is solved in such a way that others may use the solution, or the invention is in operation and proving its usefulness.

Since Wallas outlined these steps, very little improvement has been made in describing the steps involved in creativity.

MRS. LOVELACE: As you know I have four children. I'm practically sure three of them have very high I.Q.s. But the other one is different. I would guess he is above average, but in many ways he is more inventive than the others. What about the relation of I.Q. to creativity?

Intellectual Superiority and Creativity

DR. CHEAVENS: You have touched on one of the key questions about creativity. One encouraging element from the records is that one does not have to be intellectually brilliant to be creative. Of course, many of the most creative people have been intellectually superior. But many average and high average people, by measured intelligence tests, are very creative.

Everybody can become creative, with "expressive creativity." [3] It's obvious that some of these expressive creative productions will get no recognition for excellence, but the person will have had the great fun of creating, which means that life has become more zestful. From the very young and immature, from the mentally deficient, this type of creativity is all that can be expected. Give everybody, young, old, limited, superior, or deviant, an atmosphere in which creativity is stimulated.

We hear a great deal of criticism of what is sometimes broadly called "modern art." I am really for these screwball, dissociated productions. If it does the artist good to produce them, if he feels better for having done his work in his own way, while I may not want to hang his paintings on my walls, I'm still happy that he painted his picture in his own way to get the most out of it. There is room for everybody to flourish, and nearly always there will be somebody who responds to a person's creation.

MR. SHELBY: Doesn't the creative person have a hard time? Many people don't understand him. He stands out like a sore thumb.

MRS. KASTLY: Isn't that true of the person of very superior intelligence, too? He tends to be too different and people can't accept him.

DR. CHEAVENS: You're exactly right. There are both creative people and highly intelligent people that learn to adapt themselves on many levels. Some, however, don't learn this and they are the ones who have a hard time. But it is true that the reaction of many uncreative people toward the creative person leaves much to be desired.

The Creative Person and the Schools

In the past, there has been considerable fear of the creative person in our culture. He was "different," "not one of us." Our educational system fostered this rejection of the creative person, both among faculty and students. One study showing this attitude took ratings of teachers by administrative school personnel, both principals and supervisors.[6] The teachers were also given a creativity measure, an "ingenuity test." The trend was for the administrators to give low ratings to teachers who were the most creative, and high ratings to those of little creativity. Fairly recently, an investigator by the name of John Holland was interested in creativity among adolescents.[7] He found that teachers tended to rate the high I.Q., conforming, rigid student who was not creative above the nonconforming, creative students. Getzels and Jackson, two other investigators, also found this to be true.[8] Teachers "enjoyed" having the high I.Q. conforming students in their classes but not the creative. These last two investigators also found that even with parents, other traits—emotional stability, moral character, and getting along with others—were preferred in their children above creativeness.

Perhaps there is a movement away from this fear of the creative student now gaining momentum in our schools. If a student is so unfortunate as to be rigid and conforming, certainly he should have his chance to achieve. But to prize this pattern of personality is unfortunate because more tend to fit into it if it is prized. This is particularly true if at the same time the creative person is rejected. With so many differences among people in our society, so many variations of personality, can't we give everybody an equal opportunity?

While there has been a rather widespread distrust of the creative person on the part of many educators, there is also a growing awareness of the importance of creativity, not only to the individual for his own "self-actualization" but as a necessary ingredient of social progress. The increased tempo of research relating to creativity is having a stimulating effect. Many schools are beginning to provide the environment which produces creativity. This involves an attitude of recognizing and encouraging creativity on the part of administrators and teachers.

If this continues we could predict that your creative child will not have to become a rebel and be branded as a nonconformist. Again our educational process should be so flexible that new ideas, different ideas, will be both accepted and rewarded.

In Akron, Ohio, the schools are providing a creative arts center for gifted children during the summer.[9] Opportunities for the talented in art, in music, and in creative writing are offered. Classes are small, limited to twenty-five. A small fee is prerequisite to attendance. A student's high grades do not guarantee that he is creative. Many of the students who had high grades were only "conformists." However, those of average to low intelligence did not usually have the creative potential the Akron educators were looking for, although "some students with low grades proved to be creative." The second summer of this educational effort for the creative established an I.Q. of 110 as minimum for admission.

One might comment that even a small fee would eliminate some of the creative students. Also the Akron program is a highly selective one for the truly talented, and this is good as far as it goes. In the ordinary school system there should be appropriate summer educational opportunities for the average and below average, which would mean many opportunities for "expressive" creativity among students of all levels of ability.

Practically all American cities are providing limited summer school opportunities for enrichment. Classes are often not for credit, with the students' interest determining their scope and nature. These summer courses may include art, creative writing, independent reading, and scientific experiments.

In an effort to provide a challenge to creative students during the regular school year, enrichment programs within the regular classroom are sometimes provided. One of these, designed on an experimental basis, was conducted at Cedar Rapids, Iowa, with encouraging results.[10] Some gifted students achieved as high as twenty-two months above their usual yearly progress. One interesting result of this experiment was that so many of the average students in the experimental class were stimulated by enrichment to the point where their achievement was far greater than expected.

Many of the educational efforts in the past were designed for the intellectually superior student, using the measured I.Q. as the basis for selection. The newer provisions are taking into consideration the relatively new finding described above—that many students who are not superior according to I.Q. are superior creatively.

One of the leading explorers of educating for creativity, Paul Torrance of the University of Minnesota, reports that teachers can become more effective in developing the creative student through both in-service programs and college courses in teacher education, in which methods for developing creativity are taught.[11] A great deal of experimental work in this area is being done, with most encouraging results.

Dr. Torrance further reports that the stepping up of research in creativity is beginning to affect the publication of educational materials aimed specifically at developing creativity. This is true of materials in mathematics and science, as well as popular books. Also, books to develop creativity in writing and other arts are being produced for all ages. Even in the field of automated teaching, Robert Myers has developed workbook programs which take into account the stages of creative process.

Dr. Torrance warns that many problems may result from the suppression of creativity. Among these are the faulty development of self-concept, learning disabilities, behavior problems, and even serious emotional and mental disorders.[11] Certainly the person is deprived of his birthright and society is cheated out of its cultural wealth.

So things are really beginning to look more encouraging about the development of creativity in the schools. We have, of course, a very long way to go before some of these attitudes and practices permeate our entire educational structure. If your schools are not developing the creative potential of students, as a parent you might distribute information, using the references in this discussion, to bring about some improvements. Working through your P.T.A. would be very effective in helping the schools put a greater emphasis on creativity.

FOOTNOTES

1. Irving A. Taylor, "The Nature of the Creative Process," in *Creativity*, ed. Paul Smith (New York: Hastings House, 1959), pp. 52–61.

2. Abraham Maslow, *Toward a Psychology of Being* (Princeton, N.J.: P. Van Nostrand Co., 1962), pp. 127–37.

3. Graham Wallas, *The Art of Thought* (London: C. A. Watts and Co., 1946), pp. 40–60.

4. Edith Weisskopf, "Some Comments Concerning the Role of Education in the 'Creation of Creation,' " *Journal of Educational Psychology* 42 (1951), 185–89.

5. Wallas, op. cit., p. 42.

6. F. B. Jex and R. M. Merrill, *An Evaluation of the Joint Academic-Year Institute*, vols. 1 and 2, University of Utah Research Monographs (Salt Lake City: University of Utah, 1958).

7. John L. Holland, "Creative and Academic Performance Among Talented Adolescents," *Journal of Educational Psychology* 52, no. 3 (1961), 136–37.

8. J. W. Getzels and P. Jackson, *Creativity and Intelligence* (New York: John Wiley and Sons, 1962).

9. Theresa Haney, "Creativity in a Summer Arts Center," *NEA Journal*, March 1961, pp. 25–27.

10. C. Parker, "A Measured Experiment with Mentally Advanced Children," *American School Board Journal* 133 (1956), 23–24.

11. Paul E. Torrance, *Guiding Creative Talent* (Englewood Cliffs, N.J.: Prentice-Hall, 1962), pp. 196–203.

12. Ibid., pp. 125–41.

12. More About the Advantages of Creativity

DR. CHEAVENS: There are other important facts about creativity that might help you foster it in your child. We shall discover them if we ask ourselves, what kinds of homes seem to produce the more creative children? What attitude should a parent have to encourage creativity?

The story of the noted American artist Benjamin West stands out as an example of helpful parental attitudes. When Benjamin was six years old, he was once left in charge of a baby girl, a relative of the family. One of his jobs was to use a big fan to keep the flies off the child. As the boy gazed at the baby's face he was entranced and forgot about the flies.

He found pen and ink and began drawing her picture. When his mother returned and found the fan neglected and a remarkable drawing of the baby completed, she said, "Oh, Benjamin, what a beautiful picture of baby you have drawn! It looks just like her!"

From then on she encouraged Benjamin's talent. From friendly Indians she secured the basic pigments red and yellow. Indigo came from her household supplies. From the hair of the cat a paint brush was made and Benjamin began to paint. By the age of sixteen he was taking orders for portraits from the village people. Wherever he went his talent was recognized and rewarded—in New York, Italy, and finally in England, where he made his permanent home. There is little doubt that Benjamin West was precocious in his talent. Still it might never have developed had it not been for his mother's encouragement and help in providing him the materials with which to work.

How much do we know about the homes from which creative

people come? And are there any clues that you can pick up from
our present knowledge that will help you provide an atmosphere
in which creativity can flourish?

Mr. Victor has done quite a good deal of reading on this topic,
so I have asked him to bring us a report.

The Home That Fosters Creativity

MR. VICTOR: Some of the clues may be found in a study conducted by Dr. Pauline Pepinsky, researcher at Ohio State University. She investigated "productive non-conformity" in college students.[1] The method used in these studies was to select people of
recognized achievement and to go back to the antecedents of this
pattern of behavior in an attempt to discover the major underlying
factors. The purpose behind the first studies was to try to establish
the probability that certain factors in human life tend to result in
productive nonconformity. The next step was to set up experimental situations to determine if, in an experimental situation, these
same factors would result in productive nonconformity. This later
stage of the study is just beginning, and will be fully reported
when it is finished.

In the field study with nineteen college girls of recognized
achievement, many factors appeared that seemed to contribute. In
the childhood period there had been training toward independence.
There had been parental respect for achievement. There had been
encouragement for the girl to make her own choices and to experience the consequences of such choices, taking the punishing consequences of errors, and the rewards of good choices.

Pepinsky writes that "their independence seems to proceed from
an internalized, well-integrated set of standards, but these values
are not reflected in a negative and self-righteous puritanism. They
have both spontaneity and self-control; they can be alone without
discomfort, but they are able to form warm, nonexploitive attachments to others."

They understand the limitations to their behavior. They are
respectful, but not "servile" toward authority. They are willing to
conform in regard to matters of little importance, but on questions
of importance they are willing to take an independent stand and
maintain it. They regard noncomformity as an end in itself as
pointless.

The people in this study were cooperative but not slavishly
conforming. Their nonconforming was not mere rebellion, but was

directed toward values which they deemed constructive. From their backgrounds we can see that some methods of child-rearing produce interest in the welfare of others, good social relations, and patterns of nonconformity that achieve creative results.

Another study that may give us some guidelines was made of 124 homes in an Ohio community.[2] These homes were classified in several ways. One of these was: democratic-accepting homes; indulgent-accepting homes; rejecting homes. Children from the democratic-accepting homes were shown to be superior in creativity, curiosity, patience, and the ability to plan.

Mr. Shelby: You haven't mentioned anything about controlling children. I have my own ideas about this but I think we need to know.

Mr. Victor: We would like to hear your ideas about controls.

Mr. Shelby: I think the best way is to enlist cooperation. Many parents feel they have to force their children either not to do something or to do something. With my three boys we are close enough together and we get along so well that they know what I ask is reasonable and they cooperate. Sometimes I have to tell them that it will be hard for them to like what I ask them to do, but usually even that they accept. Of course, sometimes they grumble.

Mr. Victor: This really fits in with these studies, in which there were certainly controls, but not the harsh, arbitrary kinds. They were the controls that tend to produce clear and flexible thinking. There are controls that produce mechanical conformity and there are controls that encourage achievement. The question is not whether or not there shall be controls. In child-rearing, controls are indispensable. Neither is the question here one of who shall exercise the controls. In most homes this resides in the parents. There are really two important questions that we ask ourselves here: "What kind of control shall be exercised?" and "To what ends shall controls be exercised?"

In the Ohio study many rural homes were found which were "autocratic with moderate warmth." Here the children made fewer choices, originated less of their own activity, and were "told what to do more." The results from these homes were that children learned obedience and socially accepted behavior. One could predict that they would become "good citizens." This, of course, is no small achievement in an era when crime is growing apace and is increasing more rapidly percentagewise than is the population.

However, this type of control tends to result in nonproductive conformity. The children are not creative. The basic emotions producing the behavior are a combination of fear and affection. Dominating parents have created the fear of nonconformity. There has to be affection but perhaps there is a fear that if there is nonconformity, affection may be removed. This is the perfect atmosphere to produce the "Organization Man," who wishes to relate well to those with whom he is associated but who fears to disagree with them or strike out on his own even if he knows logically that it would be best to do so.

Both of the above studies reveal the type of home "control" that allows optimal development of children. One might even describe it as creative control. Since for most of the world the home still remains the basic unit of greatest importance in the development of people, it will be hard to place too much emphasis upon establishing a climate in the home that will be most favorable to the children.

Ridiculous Extremes of Conformity

DR. CHEAVENS: This fine report has given us the gist of what we need to know. It seems that we have a good many people in our culture who have grown up under the combination of dominating parents who also gave the children a reasonable amount of affection. A large number of controlled experiments have been carried out, such as those of social psychologist Crutchfield at the University of California, showing some of the ridiculous extremes of conformity among us.[3] He found this to be true not only with college students but with successful professional people such as architects and mathematicians.

Crutchfield devised a scheme in which the person would get the judgments of people whom he felt were his equals on various problems. Even though the person knew his own judgment was correct, he would often change his judgment if a group of four or five people were unanimous in judgments that disagreed with his. He was afraid of disagreeing with others. For example some quite high level mathematicians yielded to false group consensus on "fairly easy" arithmetic problems. They would record answers *they knew were wrong*, just to agree with the group!

People must be very fearful if they behave this way. And apparently it is fear like this that stifles creativity. Of course the lack of creativity shows itself not only in such slavish conformity, but also in not achieving at all. Something is sadly askew in a culture that can produce such irrational conformity!

Increasing Creative Ability

One topic in which we are all interested is whether creative achievement can be increased. If a person reaches adulthood with a record of little if any creativity, can this record improve? Can the creativity of younger people be increased? Can the schools do anything to enhance creativity?

The record from industry for increasing the productive creativity of workers is encouraging. For example, Walter J. Friess, supervisor of program development for the AC Spark Plug Division of General Motors reported that a group of engineers who went through their training program for creativity increased their output an average of 40 percent.[4] These were useful, new ideas that came as the result of training.

This company has a number of training courses designed to stimulate creativity of workers in all categories—engineers, supervisors, secretaries, and hourly employees. An effort is made to enlarge general understanding of creativity, the drives that lie behind it, what tends to block it, and how it may be released. There are specific activities provided that seem to release creative forces.

These techniques are aimed at stimulating workers to generate large numbers of ideas, without being critical of them as in Osborne's "brainstorming," which will be discussed more fully later. A second method, the "checklist" system is used to stimulate the worker to think of everything possible related to any given problem. Also there is practice in step-by-step problem-solving procedure and, on a higher level, some other methods that apply to the special needs of this industry. These methods seem to work for AC. Different procedures might be more effective for other companies. Yet the general principles would tend to be about the same.

MR. WALLACE: My company uses two methods to foster creativity. The first is Osborne's brainstorming which Dr. Cheavens mentioned.[5] A group of say fifteen or twenty people are given a problem that needs solving. They are told just to produce lots of ideas, all kinds of ideas that have anything at all to do with the problem. They are to tell their ideas, even those that seem half-baked, or ridiculous, or completely screwball. They are instructed not to sit in judgment on either their own ideas or those of others. The one big job is to produce ideas and lots of them. The aim here is to get the ideas flowing.

The second method is called the checklist method which Dr. Cheavens also named. You are given a problem to solve. You work alone. On a sheet of paper you write a list of everything that seems related to the solution. They've found that toward the last half of the list the ideas get better. It seems you warm up as you go.

DR. CHEAVENS: Thank you for giving us examples of these two methods. Of course these methods are for adults. With children what you want is to stimulate the child and to free him from the feeling that he can't produce. You create a favorable environment.

What seems to happen in brainstorming is that people who never dreamed they had good ideas begin to produce. Before, they were inhibited for many reasons—afraid of being laughed at, or because of deep feelings of inferiority. Now they find themselves free of those inhibitions and beginning to create. People are loosened up, they have a good time, and they give out numerous workable ideas. Usually stenographers are taking down everything that is said, and later it will be carefully evaluated. With many groups, including AC Spark Plug, it seems to work.

Dr. Sidney J. Parnes of the University of Buffalo writes that, in a series of reports on recent research on creativity, about half the studies "were devoted to the deliberate development of creative ability." [6]

Dr. Parnes himself has made a great contribution to the knowledge of how to develop creativity. For fifteen years he has been conducting courses in creative problem-solving at the University of Buffalo and at the same time conducting experiments in classes. He has experimented widely with Osborne's brainstorming methods. He discovered that those who had taken his course in creative problem-solving produced more and better ideas than those not taking the course. [7]

He worked also with the checklist system that Mr. Wallace talked about, in which the person works alone after being given some practical problem to solve, and is told to list all of the ideas he may have about solving the problem. As people warm up on the checklist, their ideas get better and better. More usable ideas come toward the end of the list than at the beginning. [8]

Parnes took follow-up tests on students who had taken his courses. Superiority which had been gained during the course was retained as long as eight months later. Measurement was not made beyond this point.

Previously, creativity was felt to be something almost mystical, possessed by only a few lucky people. Now we are becoming convinced that creative potential is almost universal and that the appropriate methods can develop it. Irving Maltzman, of the University of California, who has experimented widely with the process, states that "originality is a learned form of behavior." [9]

So then our evidence says that even adults can experience considerable development in creative activities. If this is true of adults, it would be reasonable to assume that the earlier one begins the development of his creative potential, the greater that development can be.

Children from affectionate families allowing considerable freedom and independence, who are stimulated by the example of others in the family toward creativity, have a distinct advantage. But apparently the schools can take children who have manifested little creativity and help them develop it. And even after one becomes an adult, the cause is not completely lost.

Some teachers have developed the skills to establish in the classroom a climate favorable to creative activity. Many teachers can learn these skills through in-service training, workshops, and other courses teaching the elements that make for creative expression of students.

My vote is cast for giving parents the information they need to provide the favorable atmosphere for creativity. Next we should expand to all the schools, and then to adults who are out of school in industry, business, and the professions.

The world needs creative people—the more the better. And people need to develop and express their creative potential. Not only is this needed, but creativity is fun, so why deny this pleasure to the people of the world?

FOOTNOTES

1. Pauline Pepinsky, "Social Exceptions that Prove the Rule," in *Conformity and Deviation*, eds. Irwin A. Berg and Bernard M. Bass (New York: Harper Bros., 1960), pp. 404–407; 387–88.

2. A. L. Baldwin, J. Kalhorn, and F. H. Breese, "Patterns of Parent Behavior," *Psychological Monographs* 58, no. 268 (Washington, D.C.: American Psychological Association, 1958).

3. Richard S. Crutchfield, "Conformity and Diversity," in *Conflict and Creativity*, eds. Seymour M. Farber and Roger H. L. Wilson, vol.

II of *Control of the Mind* (New York: McGraw-Hill, 1963), pp. 213–218.

4. Walter J. Friess, "A Case History on Creativity in Industry," in *Creativity*, ed. Paul Smith (New York: Hastings House, 1959), p. 181.

5. A. F. Osborne, *Applied Imagination* (New York: Scribner's, 1953).

6. S. J. Parnes, "Education and Creativity," *Teachers College Record* 64, no. 4 (1963), 331–39.

7. S. J. Parnes and Arnold Meadow, "Effects of brainstorming instructions on creative problem-solving by trained and untrained subjects," *Journal of Educational Psychology* 50, (1959), 171–76.

8. S. J. Parnes, "Effects of extended effort in creative problem-solving," *Journal of Educational Psychology* 52, no. 3 (1961), 117–22.

9. Irving Maltzman, S. Simon, and L. Licht, "The Persistence of Originality-training Effects," *Technical Report 4* (Washington, D.C., 1959).

13. Advantages of Good Motivation

DR. CHEAVENS: One thing we mentioned last time was stimulation—the stimulation of creativity. It relates directly to the topic chosen for this discussion—Motivation.

Many parents ask questions about motivating their children, especially about their learning at school. Parents are distressed, and this is easy to understand, when a child shows little or no enthusiasm for learning at school. The schools, of course, have a large responsibility here. They are more directly involved in school-learning. Ideally, motivating a child in school should be a cooperative job of both the school personnel and the parents.

But first let's take a look at learning apart from the environment of the school. Every child born with an average ability to think and observe is originally already equipped with strong motivation to learn. This may even be an innate quality. Some of the learning experts have concluded that it is. The normally healthy, averagely intelligent child is equipped with a great amount of curiosity.

This bountiful supply of curiosity, if encouraged, is the greatest capital you have in regard to your child's learning. Gratifying his curiosity is very satisfying to your child—it is one of the best rewards, resulting in the child's learning for the sake of learning.

The curiosity that causes a child to explore, to investigate, to inquire, is found to a certain extent in animals, too. Dr. Harlow, psychologist at the University of Wisconsin, discovered that his Rhesus monkeys would manipulate simple puzzles without requiring a reward of grapes or bananas or even the approval of their owner.[1] The monkey apparently liked to manipulate the puzzles. The activity itself was fun.

The Advantages of Intrinsic Motivation

This comes as no surprise to most parents who give their children many opportunities for learning experiences. I have seen the two children of a young couple I know well work puzzles when no one was voicing approval or giving their work any recognition. The activity in itself was rewarding. This intrinsic motivation is the best of all motivations, and much of it begins with the satisfaction of curiosity.

Dr. J. S. Bruner of Harvard has said that for the most effective learning, the child must become intrinsically motivated. He begins to learn because of his own curiosity, because he wishes to discover. He learns because the learning is its own reward. Dr. Bruner says, "Much of the problem in leading a child to effective cognitive activity is to free him from the immediate control of environmental rewards and punishments." [2] The whole question of reward and punishment deserves considerable thought and discussion, which we will postpone until later.

The opposite of intrinsic motivation is extrinsic motivation, in which there is no inherent or natural connection between the activity and the later reward. A parent offers a piece of candy if his child will clean up his room. There is no inherent connection between cleaning up the room and the piece of candy. If the child cleans up his room because he enjoys seeing it neat and orderly, he is intrinsically motivated.

As each of us looks at his own experience, intrinsic motivation seems to be the truly effective way to learn. We set out on the pathway of intellectual discovery and find an exhilaration in the experience of discovery. We wish to repeat the experience. Our quest leads us further along the same path. It leads us into other enticing paths. We tend to put together what has been learned, and to make applications and interpretations spontaneously. Our memory for what is learned by this procedure is keener and more enduring.

An experiment that indicates the advantage of the intrinsic over the extrinsic is described by Dr. Bruner. Students were given pairs of words which they were instructed to remember. One group was given merely the simple instruction. Another group was told to remember the pairs by thinking of or inventing another word that would link them together. A third group was told to learn the pairs and was given a word by the investigator that would link the two words of each pair together.

The students of the second group who provided their own way of linking the words together (intrinsic) were far superior in their learning of the material. On one run they remembered up to 95 percent of the second words in the pair, contrasted with the less than 50 percent remembered by the other children.

In discussing the relationship of intrinsic methods to memory, Bruner writes:

> One can cite a myriad of findings to indicate that any organization of information that reduces the aggregate complexity of material by imbedding it into a cognitive structure a person has constructed will make that material more accessible for retrieval. In short, we may say that the process of memory, looked at from the retrieval side, is also a process of problem solving; how can material be "placed" in memory so that it can be got on demand? . . . Let me suggest that, in general, material that is organized in terms of a person's interests and cognitive structures is material that has the best chance of being accessible in memory.

Bruner states that in extrinsically motivated learning, in which the student "gives back" what is expected of him, the learning is not related to the rest of the student's knowledge and therefore does not really become his own. Bruner proposes that learning should be discovery rather than "learning about" things. The reward, then, is not someone's approval but the thrill of discovery itself.

The role of the parent in promoting this kind of learning is to provide freedom for all kinds of investigation, and from time to time to share in the child's joy of discovery. Certainly a parent should never discourage curiosity about anything. This is rather generally done by parents who don't want to be bothered, or who feel the child is too young to find out about some things about which he asks questions. If he is old enough to ask questions, he needs the opportunity to find the honest answers.

MRS. ZIMMER: My seven-year-old is in the second grade. From the time she started school, both teachers have encouraged curiosity. She is interested in so many things she's hard to keep up with. Her questions keep me learning all the time, and the three-year-old is getting in the mood, too.

MRS. VICTOR: Our experience is mixed. The six-year-old has a wonderful teacher. He keeps them on their toes all the time. Jim is wild about school, and is learning. Last year for Wade, the nine-year-old, the teacher emphasized grades and conformity. Wade did well, but mainly because she made him.

The Problem of Intrinsic Motivation in the Schools

DR. CHEAVENS: What both of you have said shows clearly our situation today.

In the schools you will find all kinds of teaching. Generally, teaching methods seem to be improving, but we still have a very long way to go before we catch up with what we know about the best ways of teaching and learning. Some teachers use as much intrinsic motivation as they can. Others don't seem to know anything about it at all. Some teachers stimulate curiosity. Others kill it. In the past a great many parents and teachers were in the business of exterminating curiosity and did a pretty good job of it, until education became a dull monotonous thing, entirely disagreeable to the student. Fortunately, we are beginning—just beginning—to change this.

For one thing, even if a teacher is completely sold on intrinsic motivation and is skilled in using it, if the class is very large, intrinsic motivation becomes very difficult to use. And when we examine our colleges with huge lecture sections running in the hundreds and sometimes even in the thousands, the situation makes it almost impossible to use intrinsic motivation.

One of the goals we should set up in our schools is to reduce the size of classes. This means spending more money on education.

There is no way of achieving a superior educational system without investing a great deal of our wealth in it. In the long run, however, this investment will create more wealth, and most important of all will develop each person to his own capacity. Our greatest resource is people, and we should aim at their optimal development. In our country we spend more on cigarettes than on education. This is also true of our expenditures on other nonessentials such as liquor or cosmetics. Why should we hesitate to spend more on education?

Just reducing the size of classes, of course, won't insure the use of intrinsic motivation. Teachers must want to use it and be trained so that they will be skilled in using it. Learning is exhilarating. It is the land of inexhaustible adventure. Why make it dull, drab, and monotonous? Simply by capitalizing on curiosity, the adventure of discovery can enhance the entire process of education.

Another word should be added here about extrinsic motivation. While it is inferior to the intrinsic variety, still we are sometimes in situations where we have to motivate extrinsically. Certainly this is better than no motivation at all for necessary learning. Teachers with large classes do the best they can, which is mostly to use extrinsic motivation. And it gets results.

Sometimes extrinsic motivation will get a person started on a path of learning where the motivation becomes intrinsic. In teaching psychology to very large sections of college students, we use the extrinsic motivators of grades, grade points, and hours of college credit. But some students starting out with only this extrinsic motivation find the study of psychology rewarding in itself. The motivation shifts from a lower to a higher level.

Rewards and Punishment

MRS. LOVELACE: I think I have sensed all along that you are against corporal punishment. All of you know I have four children, spaced about two years apart. In some emergencies, it seems a good spank is the best thing. If nothing else it may be a time-saver. Then look at all of us. We turned out fairly well as adults and most of us were subjected to spankings and the like.

MRS. SONNEMAN: I'm not so sure I agree. Usually there is a better way. We ought to be willing to take more time with the children.

MRS. LOVELACE: You've got only two to look after. There's a difference when you double that.

MRS. ZIMMER: Living only two doors from you, I pretty well know how things go. Even if you administer an occasional spanking, you show all the children a lot of warmth and love.

MRS. SONNEMAN: Well, even if we make mistakes with our children, that warmth goes a long way toward making up for mistakes.

DR. CHEAVENS: I think we're close to agreement. Even though most of us were spanked or given corporal punishment as children, that doesn't mean it's the best way to do it. It may come as a surprise to many, but more convicted juvenile delinquents come from homes in which the parents used corporal punishment. If a parent uses punishment, it ought to be a teaching device. It should be correctional. But let's have a good look at reward and punishment in general and see what they do. I've asked Mrs. Sonneman if she can bring us a few examples of research from her study a little later.

As a parent you are interested in the effectiveness of reward and punishment, and their value in teaching your child. What we have been discussing has been largely related to reward alone. The reward of intrinsic motivation is the satisfaction that comes from the activity itself and the result of the activity. Extrinsic motivation implies some sort of external reward such as money, a good grade, or the approval of others.

With extrinsic motivation, there is often some threat of punishment. In school work there is the threat of disapproval of parents and teachers if a poor grade is made. This disapproval may range from hard to mild, but it is still punishing. Of course a bad grade in itself is punishing because it says to the student, "You did a rotten job."

In one of the earlier discussions we mentioned Dr. Sears's book *Patterns of Child-Rearing in America.*[3] In the investigation which this book reports, over 80 percent of the parents used corporal punishment on their children: spanking, slapping, ear-pulling, and other types. But most of these parents didn't think it worked very well. And they were right! In the long haul punishment is an inferior method of teaching.

MRS. LOVELACE: I know I'm wrong in saying corporal punishment is effective. But why did such a big number of these parents use it, if it did no good?

MR. VICTOR: Maybe because they didn't know what else to do, or because their own parents and grandparents used it. Just a bad habit!

MRS. LOVELACE: (with a sort of rueful laugh) Or maybe because they were unwilling to take more time, like me.

MRS. WALLACE: Some may have just taken the easy way out. With my big brood I've had to watch myself on that.

DR. CHEAVENS: It takes thought and planning to devise positive ways of teaching a child. Many parents are unwilling to give the matter that much time and thought, unfortunately.

Of course, corporal punishment is not the only kind. Verbal punishment in a harsh, disapproving voice can be sometimes more crushing and threatening than a spanking. Or still more threatening is the removal of love where the parent becomes rejecting of the child.

Let's take an example and see what we can get out of it. Mother comes home to find that Junior, four years old, has raided the jam jar, leaving telltale signs not only in the kitchen, but in both the living and dining rooms, as well as all over his clothing, hands, and face. In her understandable exasperation she gives Junior a spanking of unmistakable fervor.

Perhaps the spanking was more an outlet for her anger than a method of teaching Junior. But let us examine the punishment in the light of what Junior might have learned. First he probably learned to be more adroit in his pilfering. Next time he will cover up his tracks. From the mother's viewpoint this might have some obvious advantages since there would be less mess. However, he has begun to hide his behavior from his mother, which may not have advantages. Later, to avoid punishment, he may resort to lying. Nearly all, perhaps all, falsifying is fear-based. He has also learned to avoid his mother. He may do so more and more in the future. He has learned to be angry with his mother, and this anger may develop into habitual hostility if it should be repeated enough.

Junior has also learned that when you are angry at someone smaller than you, you may show this anger in violence. His mother did this and since she did, he may imitate her. Junior may take out his anger on smaller children by hitting them. These are a few of the learnings Junior may have received from this experience.

"But what am I to do?" asks the distraught parent. "Let him get by with it?"

No, this can be a real learning experience for Junior. Mother can sit down and explain why he should not mess things up. She might even enlist his help in cleaning up the mess. She can then explain to him that in the future when she leaves there will be a jam sandwich for him in the refrigerator to counteract his gnawing pangs of hunger.

Out of this experience Junior would learn that his mother really cares for him and his welfare—that she is on his side. He would learn that living together is a matter of cooperating. He would learn that his mother thinks him a person of worth and of intelligence, who can learn the desired behavior. His mother respects him. He respects her in return.

Just as undesirable would have been for Mother to pass the incident over without teaching Junior the appropriate behavior, or to have made excuses for him, saying that soiling the rug and the rest of the house was unimportant. Overindulgence is just as damaging in its way as harsh punishment.

MRS. WALLACE: To clear up a point. By reward you don't mean just giving him things like money or toys, do you?

DR. CHEAVENS: You are right. This would be an insult to intelligence and character.

What your child needs and wants is a warm, close relationship with his parents. With abundant affection your child will respond with affection. Cooperation is usually not difficult to secure under these circumstances. Teaching becomes effective because your child respects his parents' superiority of ability and skills. Under these circumstances your child becomes teachable.

If there is this satisfying relationship, children do not have to be "paid off" or bribed. A partnership exists in which the parent is the senior partner with authority. On this basis, behavior patterns can be worked out satisfactorily. Neither does a parent or teacher need to feel obligated to express approval of all a child's right behavior. Occasional approval is enough.

Likewise, in regard to achievement, praise does not have to be lavish, neither is it needed for every achievement. What in learning theory is called "partial reinforcement," rewarding or reinforcing just every now and then, seems to establish stronger behavior patterns than lavish, too-often-given rewards.

As a broad, general principle, we can say with assurance that reward is more effective than punishment as a teaching device. This holds true all the way from animals to humans, from the very young to those who are mature. Punishment teaches only what not to do. Reward teaches what to do. Punishment arouses anger, disappointment, and hostility. Reward results in pleasure and co-operation.

What many parents lose sight of is that so-called "discipline" should be a matter of teaching the child. And what teaches most effectively should be used. Dr. B. F. Skinner, one of the recognized authorities on learning, says that the by-products of punishment are "fear, anxiety . . . rage." [4] This would apply to scolding, spanking and the withdrawal of love. Hasn't the time come for parents to invent positive ways of teaching their children without causing anxiety and rage?

We have come to Mrs. Sonneman's report now. She has been in close touch with the research. It's very interesting to me and I think it will be to you.

Experiments on Reward vs. Punishment

MRS. SONNEMAN: Studies having to do with the effects of reward and punishment on learning date back to the early days of experimental psychology. E. L. Thorndike of Columbia was a careful, objective workman. After many experiments and studying the results of other experimenters, Thorndike came to the conclusion that reward was more effective as a teaching device than punishment. He accumulated the evidence of both animal and human experiments in a review presented in one of his volumes entitled *The Psychology of Wants, Interests, and Attitudes.*[5] This array of evidence and that of hundreds of later experiments is very convincing.

One study compared the method of showing approval for success in correctly working arithmetic problems with showing disapproval for problems solved incorrectly. Under approval for success the children learned arithmetic more rapidly than under disapproval for their failures.[6] And the disapproval was only a very mild punishment!

A similar study with college students used two learning tasks. Students who were encouraged did much better than students who were discouraged. In this experiment there was a surprise—students who were neither encouraged nor discouraged did worst of all![7] Apparently one of the most demoralizing of all attitudes toward people is to ignore them. We remember from our studies of maternal deprivation in an early discussion, that neglected children were more subject to disease, to deviant and subnormal behavior than children who were not neglected.

The two examples given above used punishment that could be classified as rather mild, and the rewards were simple verbal rewards of approval. In cases where harsh punishment is used, the damage to human beings is incalculable.

One point on which authorities agree is that punishment does not really weaken a response. It merely suppresses it until a more favorable opportunity for expression presents itself—and then watch out! There is some evidence to indicate that punishment may even strengthen an undesirable response. Even with suppression of the response, evidence points to the fact that the effects are not very lasting.

Worst of all the effects of punishment are the emotions aroused in the punished. He becomes angry with the punisher and may even come to dislike him strongly. The punished person may also suffer a great loss of self-respect and feel he is a bad person and unworthy of love and respect.

DR. CHEAVENS: With all this evidence, it comes as no surprise that Mrs. Sonneman is no advocate of corporal punishment.

A very great deal of our motivation in school-learning is based on the fear of punishment. True, schools no longer use the harsh, violent beatings that they once used. So we have made some progress. But why does the child do his school work? In great part because he fears disapproval of teacher, of parents, and sometimes of friends. There is a threat hanging over the head of the student all the time. He may make a bad grade! Then mother and dad will disapprove. At times the entire school-learning process is associated with threat and the learning process becomes extremely unpleasant because of this association. This may account for the dislike so many students have for school. Associate any process for long with threat and the process itself becomes threatening.

All the way from home to school to the working world, we should strive for the greater use of intrinsic motivation. Where this is not practical, let's avoid the use of punishment (except maybe in a few emergencies) and intelligently devise ways of periodically rewarding desirable behavior.

FOOTNOTES

1. H. F. Harlow, M. K. Harlow, and D. R. Meyer, "Learning Motivated by a Manipulation Drive," *Journal of Experimental Psychology* 40, (1950), 228–34.

2. J. S. Bruner, "The Act of Discovery," *Harvard Educational Review* 31 (1961), 21–32.

3. R. R. Sears, et al., *Patterns of Child Rearing* (Evanston, Ill.: Row, Peterson and Co., 1957), pp. 328–31.

4. B. F. Skinner, *Science and Human Behavior* (New York: The Macmillan Company, 1953), p. 184.

5. E. L. Thorndike, *The Psychology of Wants, Interests, and Attitudes* (New York: Appleton-Century-Crofts, 1935), pp. 135–44; 248–55.

6. E. B. Hurlock, "An Evaluation of Certain Incentives Used in School Work," *Journal of Educational Psychology* 16 (1925), 145–59.

7. G. S. Gates and L. Rissland, "The effects of encouragement and discouragement upon performance," *Journal of Educational Psychology* 14 (1923), 21–26.

14. Advantages of Developing According to Individuality

Dr. Cheavens: In helping people, Dr. Alfred Adler was always looking for what he called each person's "life-style." Your child has his own unique life-style. And only if he follows this will he develop to his optimum.

Every Individual Is Unique

One of our greatest needs is to treat each individual in the world as a unique personality. Even identical twins are different. Nearly always one is physically stronger than the other, and one is more intelligent, although identical twins reared in the same home tend to be closer together in these respects than other children. Nearly always one twin is dominant or the leader.

Good parents try never to show partiality to children but to give one child about the same treatment as the other. This is fine. But it is another matter to expect Mary to be good in math just because Jane was—or to expect Jack to be interested in football just because Joe was.

Mrs. Zimmer: It seems to me even identical twins are different. I have identical twins as neighbors. Right away I picked out small differences in appearance so I could tell them apart. Then I began to notice their different ways of behaving.

Dr. Cheavens: I think that is a commentary not only on the twins but on you. Not many people are as observant as that. In a moment I would like to comment on differences in identical twins.

Children are born different, with different temperaments, different abilities. As they begin to develop, these differences become more marked. Environmental forces have much to do with shaping the child, but no two children, not even identical twins, have the same environment.

Let's look at identical twins, A and B. What is their social environment. Suppose they are the only children and live with both parents. A's primary social environment in the home is Mother, Father, and twin B. B's home social environment is Mother, Father and twin A. As they grow older Mother begins to respond differently to A than to B and so does Father. Twin B tends to be more aggressive and dominant than A. A tends to be more submissive and affectionate. So twin A has an aggressive twin in his environment and twin B has a more submissive twin in his. You can see how, as this continued, the environments of each twin would become different. The social is perhaps the most important part of the environment, anyway.

The Problem of Individual Differences in School

The point is that all people are born different and no two people ever have the same environment. Neither do they ever have the same heredity, although we say that identical twins do. And yet we put all six-year-olds in the first grade and sometimes expect them all to make the same progress in the same subjects at the same time. We treat them as if they were all cut from one pattern. This is most unrealistic.

Here is a child that learns slowly. Yet he is expected to keep up the same pace as all the others. Here is another who learns very rapidly, and we sometimes expect him to fit the learning pattern of the average child. In the first case the child may feel that he is not measuring up to expectations. He is ashamed of himself and begins to feel he is out of place. In the other case the child may rebel at being held back and expected to be average.

MR. VICTOR: The son of one of our friends was in a seventh grade class. Marvin is exceptionally bright. The social studies teacher announced that they were going to begin to study Indians.

Marvin went up to her after class and said, "Mrs. X, I've been studying Indians since before I started school. I won't mind doing a study on Indians if you will let me do an exhaustive study on

one tribe. I would enjoy going to the anthropological and histori-
cal journals and doing a lot of research on, say, the Tonkewa
Indians that lived in this area."

Marvin's request took Mrs. X by surprise. Her reaction was
defensive, because she felt threatened by this superior student.
"No Marvin," she told him, "you must learn to conform. You must
study Indians along with the rest of the class in the same way they
do."

For the first time in his life Marvin became a behavior problem,
and is there any wonder? Finally, he had to be transferred out of
Mrs. X's class.

DR. CHEAVENS: This is a good example of the superior student. The slow student, on the other hand, is also expected to
keep up with the average. He feels the disapproval of his parents,
his kin, perhaps of his fellow-students, and of his teacher. He
begins to feel that he can't learn at all and that he can't achieve
at all. He becomes hopeless about himself.

I had the good fortune to work as a consultant for the Job Corps
Conservation Centers several summers ago. Practically all the
Job Corps boys in these Centers were school drop-outs. Many of
them are slow learners and fit into the description above.

Part of the program of these Centers is school work. The work
is planned so that the student *goes at his own speed.* Many of
these boys who felt they couldn't learn, found out they could.
When they did, some of them couldn't get enough of school. The
teachers usually tried to give the boys a break about every half
hour. I've seen many of these boys so interested in learning that
they wouldn't take a break at all. Of course, the material was programmed for individual work.

It isn't only a matter of letting a person work at his own speed,
but of letting him *work on his own level.* In both reading and
arithmetic most books are graded—preprimer, primer, first grade,
and so on. In reading, these classifications mean the level of difficulty of the language. In order to read the usual fifth grade book
a student usually must read a number of fourth grade books, and
before that, third and second and first. In arithmetic the grade
levels involve problems of a complexity which require knowledge
from former levels of learning. At least this is the general idea
in progressing from one level to another.

Usually there would be no point in starting a student in a fourth
grade book if he is reading on a second grade level. It would be
just as foolish as telling a man who is building a brick wall, "Now
I want you to start with row four."

But in many schools, just because a student is nine years of age, he is expected to read in a fourth grade book, and to work successfully arithmetic problems in a fourth grade book.

Adapting to the Needs of the Individual

Fortunately many of our schools now are adapting the work to the ability of the student. Conceivably, in the fourth grade you might have a student who would be reading on a primer level and another student of the same age who needs eighth grade books.

The point is that if we are to succeed in educating people we have to adapt the learning task to the student. Our educational system should become so flexible that it adapts itself to the needs of any and all students, the slow, the fast, the average, the conformer, the nonconformer, the uncreative, and the creative. We should take every person right where he is in his learning progress, retarded or advanced, and let him proceed on his own road of development at his own speed, slow or fast or average.

MRS. DANA: The junior high school my thirteen-year-old goes to has what they call ability-grouping. They do it according to achievement scores in reading and math.

MRS. LOVELACE: Does that mean if they get in one group they're stuck there?

MRS. DANA: No, it doesn't. They'll transfer a student any time it's recommended. If the student is gaining rapidly he is put in a faster group. If he can't do the work well, he's put in a slower group. It works fine in this school.

MRS. LOVELACE: Don't the students in the slow groups feel they're dumbbells or stupid?

MRS. VICTOR: If it was a mixed group with superior, average, and slow students, wouldn't the slow feel the same thing?

MRS. DANA: I think Mrs. Victor is right. Being able to move makes a lot of difference. I hear that the slow groups are ashamed of being where they are, but as Mrs. Victor says, the slow would feel inferior anywhere they're put. Generally this plan works well. James is interested in school and the others with him are too. They do very advanced work.

DR. CHEAVENS: Any system will have disadvantages. Many schools use ability grouping in some form. As Mrs. Dana suggested, it should never be rigid.

If the class size is small, the teacher may be able to direct each child individually, although usually some group work is possible. With a class of fifteen children, there might be three very slow ones working at about the same level and two or three who are very advanced. The others might fall loosely into one average group.

There are a number of ways to get the job done. The chief thing is to get it done and to remember that we must adapt the materials of education to the individual, not the individual to the materials.

Programmed Instruction

One fairly new development on the educational scene may give us some help. It goes by various names—programmed instruction, automated teaching, or teaching machines.

Certainly it is not advocated here that programmed instruction take the place of a well-informed, skillful teacher working with a group of students. But the programmed instruction can supplement the teacher's work. And in some cases it can relieve the teacher of some of the drudgery of teaching.

Where no teachers can be employed, for whatever reasons, programmed instruction can be made available to enable people to learn whatever they need to learn, all the way from a foreign language to a mathematical skill. Each person can have a private tutor available, a robot teacher. A person alone in the wilderness will be able to master areas of learning in his isolation.

The advantages of programmed instruction are clear. Each person can learn at his own speed, all the way from very rapidly to very slowly. The learner must be active, not passive, in the learning process. The learner is given immediate feedback, or knowledge of his progress. He knows whether he is "getting it" or not. Activity and feedback are two major essentials for effective learning. Without them learning is not very efficient.

Already, experimental evidence is mounting to show the good results of programmed learning. For example, elementary school children were taught spelling on teaching machines on the second and sixth grade levels.[1] The purpose, in the experimental groups, was to cover about the same amount of material as taught in the old way to children in control groups which were matched for learning ability with the experimental children.

Measurement at the end of the year was by means of standardized achievement tests. The students who used automated instruction were easily superior to the control children taught by the usual methods.

One very notable result from this experiment was that children with higher I.Q.s didn't do much better than children of lower I.Q.s in the groups using teaching machines. We must keep in mind that this was spelling, a fairly simple skill.

Also we have to be careful about results such as these because sometimes just the newness of the method means the students will perform better. However, some industries have discovered that most of their teaching of certain skills can be of the programmed type, saving time, energy, and money. This is a practical indication that we can accept.

In the groups not using the teaching machines, the high I.Q. students were far ahead of the lower I.Q. students. This probably means that if we use the right kind of programming, students of lower intelligence will be able to master some types of material which before was considered too hard for them.

With very young children, results have been promising. Fine discrimination of eyesight is a necessary part of reading readiness. One investigator showed that teaching machines were successful in developing visual discrimination in preschool children.[2] Also, six-year-olds were taught by J. G. Holland, then research fellow at Harvard, to reason inductively, using programmed instruction. Children with speech defects were taught to discriminate sounds, with rapid improvement in their pronunciation of these sounds.

Part of an extensive study in the schools of Roanoke, Virginia, was the programmed instruction in algebra of eighth grade students who covered two semesters' work in one, working at school fifty minutes daily, with no homework and no help from a teacher. On a final examination over the course, 41 percent of these eighth graders were better than ninth graders who had taken the course by the old method, during two full semesters. Since the introduction of programmed math courses there has been a substantial reduction of failures in math in the Roanoke schools.

In elementary schools fourth and fifth grade students scored much higher after programmed instruction than carefully matched groups learning by the usual conventional methods. Results like these were observed in teaching spelling to both second and seventh grade students with teaching machines.

In Pittsburgh, high school physics classes learned optics with the aid of teaching machines. More than 400 students in fifteen schools were in this experiment and proved to be superior to control classes taught by conventional methods.

Results from programmed courses in college have been in agreement with results in elementary and high schools. At Hamilton College students covered a course in logic in two-thirds the usual time with an increase in average grades. At UCLA a well-controlled study was conducted in teaching probability to 186 engineering students. The students taught by the machines scored much higher than a matched group of students taught by the usual methods.

As we said before, industry and business are consistently finding out how useful programmed instruction is. General Telephone Company of California, I.B.M., Bell Telephone Laboratories, DuPont, Eastman Kodak, American Radiator, Zenith, Quaker Oats, and Prudential Life are a few who have reported remarkable success in a great variety of courses taught to thousands of employees.

These results are most encouraging. Certain skills necessary in our present world can be learned well by both the average and the slow with automated teaching. Taught by conventional methods, these students might often fall behind. Morale would sag and they wouldn't do their work as well. Discouraged, many times they would tend to drop out. And the skill they need so much might never be learned.

Of course, you and I know that teaching machines can't work miracles. Everybody can go only so high. There is a ceiling to anybody's ability. But so many times we are far below that limit, and never work to our real capacity. Perhaps the programmed instruction can help us reach our capacities.

Harvard's Dr. Skinner comments on the reactions of the old-fashioned teacher to automated teaching that the method may be viewed with alarm because it maximizes success and minimizes failure.[3] About the traditional teacher, Skinner writes, "He has found that students do not pay attention unless they are worried about the consequences of their work. The customary procedure has been to maintain the necessary anxiety by inducing errors." Again we are faced with the results of using punishment or rewards as motivation in education!

Programmed courses and teaching machines make learning easier, says Dr. Skinner. "There is no evidence that what is easily learned is more readily forgotten." There is considerable evidence that what is pleasant is better remembered.[4] If learning is constantly associated with worry, the learning process becomes unpleasant and memory may get worse. Perhaps this accounts for the poor memories of lots of people who have been the victims of an educational system based upon unpleasantness.

MR. VICTOR: Don't we know, too, from a lot of evidence, that all our reasoning processes are interrupted by too much tension?

DR. CHEAVENS: As you say, we have plenty of evidence that the efficiency of reasoning and problem-solving are hindered by excess tension, or fear.[5] Anxiety produces stereotyped thinking. A person must have a great deal of flexibility if he does well with solving problems. Maybe this gives us another clue to the failure of so many people to reason accurately. Our reasoning processes have been associated with fear and anxiety for so many years that we are automatically tense when we even try to reason. The excess tension keeps our thinking from being flexible and the problem is not solved accurately. Programmed learning may help relieve the student of the nagging worry that has gone with learning in the past. And maybe it will help some of our teachers to see how foolish it is to punish people for not learning, because the threat of bad grades, or of disapproval of parents, friends, and teachers is real punishment.

Limitations of Programmed Learning

Programmed learning has its drawbacks, as you can well imagine. A person works alone to do his learning, so the social element is limited. This can be offset by having groups of students who are covering the same basic material meet with the teacher to discuss what they have learned, if it is that kind of material, or ways of applying what they've learned to everyday life situations.

Also the stimulating effect of a good teacher is absent if the student is working only with a machine. However, not all teachers are stimulating and the material itself can be made stimulating. As it stands now not all programmed material is stimulating. I think it could always be made stimulating. We have observed that there is considerable stimulus in the learner just knowing he's getting it, that he's making progress.

Anyway, this is something parents can consider for their children. Parents can also use their influence for the judicious use of programmed instruction in the schools, as an adjunct to other approaches. In some cases parents can help their own children by finding programmed courses for them.

What we can say in summing up is that education to be effective must take into account that children are different; that every child must go at his own pace and work on his own level; that the child must be active in the learning process to get the most out of it; that his learning should be rewarding in itself and that he should get knowledge of results frequently for the process to be effective. These goals are not unattainable. They are practical and if reached will improve the effectiveness of education immeasurably.

FOOTNOTES

1. Eugene Galanter, *Automatic Teaching* (New York: John Wiley and Sons, 1959), pp. 85–90.

2. J. L. Hughes, *Programmed Instruction for Schools and Industry* (Chicago: Science Research Associates, 1962), pp. 43–50.

3. B. F. Skinner, "Teaching Machines," *Science* 128 (October 24, 1958), 969–79.

4. H. Meltzer, "Individual Differences in Forgetting Pleasant and Unpleasant Experiences," *Journal of Educational Psychology* 21 (1930), 339–409.

5. E. L. Cowen, "The Influence of Varying Degrees of Psychological Stress on Problem-Solving Rigidity," *Journal of Abnormal and Social Psychology* 47 (1952), 512–19; idem, "Stress Reduction and Problem-Solving Rigidity," *Journal of Consulting Psychology* 16 (1952), 425–38.

15. Advantages of Positive Emotional Development

MRS. KASTLY: A number of us have been talking it over, and we think one period is going to be too short to cover the topic of our children's emotions. Could we take a full two periods for this?

DR. CHEAVENS: I think the extra period is necessary. If we have no objections we will decide now to extend the discussion to two periods.

A great deal of children's behavior is determined by emotion. Since this is true, what can be done about your children's emotions, and since your own emotions so directly affect your children, what can be done about your emotions?

We have already spoken about emotion from time to time in previous discussions. In the first chapter you may remember that we discussed the pregnant woman's need to be as happy as possible during pregnancy, and how important it is for her not to have long-drawn-out periods of anger, fear, anxiety, or depression.

But in this chapter we should go into more detail about emotions and how to direct them constructively. There is a bodily basis for emotion. We are born with the capacity for emotion. But very early in life the learning process begins to shape the way we express our emotions.

MRS. PUTNAM: The other discussion on emotions during pregnancy has helped me a lot. I hope these two will give me another boost.

MRS. WALLACE: Since Mrs. Putnam and I are in the same fix and I don't want her to feel all alone (laughter), I can say the same thing.

Emotions are Contagious

DR. CHEAVENS: One of the reasons why this subject of the emotions is so important, besides helping pregnant mothers, is that emotions are so easily communicated from parents to children. Your fears, your worries, your anger, your sadness, your optimism and joy all quickly affect your children. Habitual emotional reactions of parents may become the emotional habits of the children, because many children identify closely with the parents.

One father I knew had the habit of closing the shades as it grew dark, always saying, "Somebody might be looking in." Later the daughter, even in hot weather, was afraid to go to sleep with either windows or shades open. She frequently said she saw faces looking in at the window. Is it any wonder?

Nearly everyone can look back on his childhood and recall how the emotions of parents affected him. I can remember how my parents' worries and pessimism about finances influenced me and depressed me. Yet my parents would not have done anything consciously which they felt was harmful to their children.

Body Reactions During Emotion

Before we go any further, let's look at some of the things that happen in the body when a person experiences an emotion. First let's look at fear and anger.

Suppose you are walking along the sidewalk and suddenly a big dog jumps out at you. His bark is loud and threatening. His appearance is threatening too. Perhaps he won't really attack you, but you still experience fear. Your eyes and ears send a message to your brain. Your brain quickly sends messages to the rest of your body, which begins quickly to act. The adrenal glands, especially the adrenal medulla or inner part, send an extra amount of adrenalin into the blood stream. Your liver sends glycogen, a type of sugar for quick energy, into the blood stream. Your breathing gets faster, your heart beats faster, and the blood supply to the digestive system becomes small. There are also a large number of other bodily reactions.

A good many years ago, a medical researcher by the name of Walter B. Cannon published the results of research leading to a knowledge of the physiology of many of the emotions.[1] Since then we have increased our knowledge with some fairly recent important breakthroughs.

Just a few years ago, a series of experiments demonstrated that there are some fundamental differences between the physiology of fear and that of anger.[2] But in either case the important practical thing for parents to realize is that you have a sort of chain reaction in the body. Whenever the child feels threatened, which would include most frustrations, his body responds automatically to the situation. Threat of any kind triggers off the responses and what happens after is automatic. An entire set of inner bodily responses takes place. It's like throwing in a switch which sets all the machinery of a factory in motion. In fact, the body is a factory and, under threat, it puts out a number of products that may or may not be useful. There is a fundamental difference, though. When you cut off the switch in a factory, the machines stop. It doesn't quite happen that way in the human body. If the threat is removed, the reactions may not be as strong or as long, but there will be certain bodily products still demanding to be used.

If the body has been prepared for action, it really needs to go into action of some kind. One way of reducing fear is to act. An action that would either remove or reduce the threat would certainly help reduce the fear. If you run away from the barking dog and get completely away from him, your fear is reduced because the threat is removed but also because your body used up some of the energy products that fear gave.

If you didn't get into action, those unused products in your body would tend to make you more fearful in other situations that might follow. We have record of controlled experiments that show this to be true. But also if you look at your own experience you will see how it works. After the fright with the dog you would be more prone to start worrying about your children, even if there wasn't anything to worry about.

There are times when we can't get into the type of action that will remove the threat that caused our fear. We get news that some cherished member of the family is dangerously ill. We are gripped with fear, but we are in no position to remove the threat. In such a case, any vigorous exercise, like cleaning house, or walking, or pulling weeds will take the sharp edge off of fear. The emotion of fear prepares the body for action, and if the body goes into action of almost any kind, fear may not be completely done away with, but its effects are greatly reduced.

This is the way to help a child learn how to deal with his own fear—teach him that if he gets into action, fear is weakened. One mother helped her ten-year-old daughter overcome stage fright this way. The daughter was fearful of making book-reports or any sort of talk in public. The mother showed her daughter that by taking an active part in games before her book-report, she felt much calmer. When the teacher was taken into confidence, she would allow this student to go to the gym for several minutes of running or other vigorous exercise. This was the beginning of conquering stage fright.

MRS. LOVELACE: Isn't the element of distraction one of the benefits of getting into other activities? If you get active you get your mind off your fear and the cause of your fear. Anyway, from working with my children I know it works, which is the main point.

DR. CHEAVENS: This business of distracting the mind is, as you say, important. Akin to distraction is the fact that you are setting up a process of positive thinking, feeling, and acting rather than a negative one.

The bodily products of anger are somewhat different from those of fear, but the body reacts similarly to both stimuli, preparing for action. And often anger and fear are mixed. A person makes an unkind remark about us. This is a threat. First there is a fear reaction to the threat, then an anger reaction toward the inconsiderate person. At any rate, in anger you have a sort of automatic chain reaction with bodily processes and products which prepare the body to attack. Physical attack is usually not advisable, yet the bodily products remain, demanding to be used in action.

If they are not used, the angry person may vent them against people unrelated to the cause of his anger. The business man after dealing with difficult customers all day may take it out on his wife. The mother who becomes angry at another woman may take it out on her children. The child who becomes angry at his parents and does not express it, may take it out on the other children at school. He would be less prone to do this if he rode his bicycle fast to school pedalling twelve or fifteen blocks.

Emotions and Digestion

An important part of what happens in the body during emotional reactions is the effect of anger and fear on the digestive system. You just can't digest your food very well if you are either angry or afraid. Parents often worry because their children don't seem to be eating a good meal, and put pressure on the child to eat. The child begins to react to the pressure. For one thing he may not be hungry—he has been eating too much between meals or had too many cold drinks laden with sugar. Or he may not be well. Many times, when the child won't eat, he doesn't need the food. But supposing he did need the food. If he rebels against the parents' pressure to eat, there is a scene—he is spanked, made to leave the table, or otherwise punished for not eating—and the child's anger flares.

How ridiculous this is! The parents' behavior is defeating itself. Suppose the parent triumphs and the child does eat. In his emotional upset, his digestion is not going to function properly. Eating may be the worst thing he could do at this time. What goals have been reached by this parental behavior? Everyone is unhappy. The meal has become a disgusting, unpleasant scene. The purposes of eating have been completely defeated. And if this sort of thing becomes habitual, the child's unpleasant associations with eating may become very damaging to the whole process of assimilating food for the strength of the body. The groundwork is being laid for all sorts of digestive disturbances.

Let's give the parents credit for wanting the child to eat plenty of good nourishing food. This is important! But this isn't the way to get the job done! The goal isn't reached this way. The only goal that is reached by the pressure method is that everyone is upset. No one enjoys the meal. And no one digests or assimilates his food very well.

Digestion and assimilation of food take place best when the child is relaxed and happy. Eating should be a pleasure. It is much more important for mealtime to be a happy time than for the children to eat their food! And if it is made a happy time, over the long haul the child will eat enough food and get plenty of nutrition. Of course, the right food must be set before him.

Not only do fear and anger cause trouble, but digestion does not function very well either if people are sad. The physiology of depression is a slowing down of bodily processes. When people are happy the bodily processes are working smoothly and efficiently. But almost everything functions below par during depression. I think it is significant that one of the symptoms accompanying serious depression is constipation. Certainly this doesn't mean that all constipation is caused by depression. But joy and gladness are good for all the bodily processes. So the meal should be a happy time. This is more important than the amount of food eaten!

MR. SHELBY: I think the thing I am most interested in is what practical thing a father or mother can do when the child gets emotionally upset.

What You Can Do About Your Child's Emotions

Dr. Cheavens: We have been thinking about what happens in the body when people are afraid, angry, or depressed. Mr. Shelby's interest perhaps is the most important of all. What can the parent do when the children are caught by these emotions?

Let's look for a moment at the way most of us well-meaning parents react to the emotions of our children. The child is angry. We say, "Don't be angry!" Or he is afraid and we say, "Don't be afraid!" Or he is sad and we say, "Don't be sad!"

When we react this way to the child's emotions, we mean well, but how much good does it do? Really, it does hardly any good. Let's remember that those chain reactions have been set up in the child's body and the parent making these negative statements is not going to stop the chain reaction with commands.

What is going to help? There are three steps in helping, though all three may not always be necessary. They are: Recognize the emotion for what it is. Accept it as natural. Teach the child to channel the expression of his emotion constructively.

Seven-year-old Tommy has a sharp disagreement with a little neighbor girl, Suzy. He comes running home to tell mother about it. He needs to talk about it. Instead of mother's saying "You mustn't be angry at Suzy," she says, "Suzy made you very angry. Would you like to tell me all about it?"

When the mother does this she is teaching the child that being angry is no crime, and that he has freedom to express his anger in words, which is usually preferable to physical violence or just trying to hold it in. She is also showing Tommy that he can always talk freely about his emotions with her. She recognizes and accepts his emotions. He can communicate with his mother about how he feels. It is very important for parents to keep the channels of communication with their children as open as possible.

Many times Tommy will get over his "mad" quickly if he can express it fully and freely to someone who understands. After this expression he may run back over to play with Suzy quite happily. Of course, there are times when the problem is more complicated. Then the mother may say, "Well, what do you think you ought to do about that?" She is helping him solve his own emotional and social problems and expressing her confidence that Tommy can do this successfully. Or, on occasion, she might make a suggestion for the solution of the problem.

In such a case it is nearly always good policy to make two or three suggestions and let Tommy choose one to try out. Again Tommy is learning to make his own choices and solve his own problems.

But suppose it becomes necessary for either the mother or father to tell Tommy that he positively cannot do something he very much wants to do, and Tommy reacts with anger toward them?

MR. INMAN: I think I can help answer that question with a practical example. We have a neighbor who does the best job of reacting to emotional upsets of anyone I know. If Tommy is very angry, as you describe, she would say, "I know this may make you angry and you can tell me how you feel, but this is the way it has to be." The parent is still recognizing that for the child to feel angry is perfectly natural. The child does not feel that something terrible is going to happen because he experiences anger due to frustration. The child usually tells her exactly how mad he is and then he does what he is supposed to do. I've tried it with my boys and it helps a lot. At first when they told me how they felt, I found it hard to take. Now I know they're helped by it, and the whole situation is changed—I'm no longer bothered by what they say.

DR. CHEAVENS: This bears out what we've been talking about and gives us one practical method that Mr. Shelby was asking for.

FOOTNOTES

1. Walter B. Cannon, *Bodily Changes in Pain, Hunger, Fear and Rage* (New York: The D. Appleton Century Company, 1936).
2. Daniel H. Funkenstein, "The Physiology of Fear and Anger," *Scientific American* 192 (1955), 74–80.

16. More Advantages of Positive Emotional Development

Dr. Cheavens: We closed our last meeting with Mr. Shelby's request for practical methods of responding to your child's emotions and a practical example given by Mr. Inman. Perhaps tonight we'll have more of these practical methods.

Parents Can Set An Example

By the parents' reactions to him, the child begins to learn that one way he can deal with his anger is to express it in words. The parent can also teach the child that a good way of reducing anger is by some sort of physical activity. This can be done in many ways. One of them is by example.

Suppose someone makes you angry. You may have expressed it in words, and then in front of your children you say, "I'm now going out to mow the lawn. Do you know why?" And of course they will want to know why. "Because after I work hard, I won't feel so mad. I don't want to be mad." You recognize and accept your anger and you show how to direct it constructively, and how to reduce it. Children can learn this sort of thing just as they can learn to read, and it is just as important.

Fear reactions should be dealt with in somewhat the same way. Fear needs to be recognized and accepted. It is usually reduced if we talk about it openly. And moving into some sort of intelligent action helps take care of the products of fear in the body.

Mr. Shelby: I think that's one I'm going to use. Sounds like it will work.

Mrs. Sonneman: From my experience, it seems to me giving the child reasons for your behavior and for your asking him to do something helps a lot.

Mrs. Wallace: Suppose the child is too young to understand the reasons?

Mrs. Sonneman: That can very well be. In Ruth, my little one, I've watched this. Even if she couldn't understand the reasons, she seemed to get good from the fact that I was trying to explain things to her.

Mr. Inman: It let her know you were right with her and wanting her to understand.

Dealing With Causes

Dr. Cheavens: Naturally, with both anger and fear a parent can do much to help the child know that by dealing with the actual causes for these emotions, a problem can be solved. The cause of anger or fear is a problem to be solved, and also the emotion itself is a problem to be solved.

While getting at causes may be helpful, the too analytical parent may be denying the child the free verbal expression of emotion. I was once visiting a home where I was considered almost a member of the family. Mary, the fourteen-year-old daughter, came in sobbing after a humiliating experience in her club meeting. For fifteen minutes the father tried to get her to analyze why the thing had happened. Mary kept right on sobbing and talking at the same time. When Dad had a telephone call I said to Mary, "This hurt you a lot, didn't it?" She laid her head on my shoulder and cried freely and I responded in a way that let her tell me fully how she felt. This was all she really needed, and before Dad returned her tears were dried and she had gone on to something more interesting. She didn't need a careful analysis of her trouble, she needed a shoulder to cry on and someone to talk to.

Mr. Shelby: I think your account has another point, too. None of us likes to be preached to.

Dr. Cheavens: The emotion of sadness is many times caused by some disappointment or loss. Sadness, too, should be freely verbalized. Shedding tears may help, if it is not carried to an extreme, because crying and tears are outlets for sadness. So again, the emotion is recognized, accepted, and freely expressed.

Crying becomes tabu behavior for boys at a very early age in our culture. For girls we are much more permissive, but as they grow older the crying is usually done quietly and only under special circumstances. So with both boys and girls some other outlet for sadness must be found.

Beyond this the parent can teach the child to cope with the causes for loss or disappointment. Not all of them can be coped with. A friend is killed in an accident. Nothing can bring the friend back. Grief is expressed and the loss must be accepted.

If the accident could have been avoided this should be pointed out to the child. In this respect, the child is learning to cope with the causes for sorrow. But sometimes there appears to have been no way of avoiding the loss. Then express the sorrow freely and as soon as possible try to replace the loss. If this was the loss of a friend, one must of course try to find another satisfying friendship.

If the house burned down, could it have been avoided? This should be pointed out clearly, but one also begins to build another house, or take steps in that direction.

Guilt Feelings—Destructive or Constructive

Sometimes the emotion of depression, or blueness, may not be caused by some loss which can easily be identified, but by the person's feeling bad about himself and blaming himself. He experiences guilt and begins to punish himself. We say he becomes intropunitive.

Guilt feelings have their practical uses. If a child does something harmful to others he should feel guilt. This guilt may prevent him from harming someone in the future. The guilt becomes a built-in mechanism that helps him avoid undesirable behavior. This we discussed rather fully when we were talking about internalizing a code of conduct.

But excessive guilt, particularly about trivial things, can be very harmful. Suppose the child feels excessive guilt about being angry with his parents, which is a perfectly normal reaction. This can later become the basis for a troublesome depression.

I know a young woman who went through a bad period of depression. When she was a small child, she and her mother lived alone. Her mother made her feel insecure by a constant threat of withdrawing love. Every time the child felt any rebellion toward her mother, there arose painful feelings of guilt and also a fear of losing her mother's affection. The girl finally arrived at the place

where she would never resist her mother in anything. She became
overcompliant and overdependent but there was always a deep
feeling of resentment along with this submissiveness.

When the daughter reached adulthood she was still dominated
by her mother, but the daughter now wished for independence.
However, any move in the direction of opposing her mother
caused the girl intense anxiety and depression. She felt she was a
terrible person to want to act independently or to feel any rebellion
against her mother at all. From this feeling of being a "bad girl"
she became extremely depressed.

Again, a feeling of anger, even toward one's parents, should be
recognized and accepted. The child should not feel a terrible
burden of guilt about this. But there are all sorts of ways of expressing this anger. The child can be taught the appropriate and
constructive ways of expressing anger.

MR. WALLACE: We all want our children to develop self-
control. I know that a lot of the old ideas about self-control are no
longer considered very good. But we still want our children to
have workable controls.

DR. CHEAVENS: Every child must also learn to inhibit and that
may be part of what you mean by control. A wholesome type of
control includes recognizing the emotion for what it is, accepting
it as natural, and then channeling the expression of it. Channeling
can be done appropriately or inappropriately. The child can certainly find adequate release for anger or fear in the appropriate
verbal expression. For example, most parents would consider the
use of obscene or profane language to be inappropriate or in bad
taste. The child learns to use language which is in good taste even
to express anger or fear. Channeling any behavior constructively
would certainly be control.

The Principle of Substitution

You may be wondering about this business of substituting
positive thoughts for negative thoughts, positive action for negative action, positive emotions for negative emotions. Isn't this a
sound principle?

Yes, it is. But in each case there should be a clear recognition
of the negative nature of the emotion, thought, or action. What
is to be gained by a denial that it is there and that it is negative?
Nothing. After it is recognized for what it is, and expressed
freely, then the principle of substitution is certainly the next step.

The child learns to recognize anger and then to substitute a constructive way of expressing it rather than a destructive one.

The child recognizes fear for what it is. He expresses it and does whatever he can about it. He can deal with his fear more positively if he sees it clearly and understands what caused it. Likewise with sadness or depression, the child learns to see it clearly and understand it. Expressing it usually helps to get rid of it. Doing something about the cause helps to get rid of the sadness.

In each case the goal is to free oneself from the negative and establish the positive. We learn to deal with anger so that we will feel good will and friendliness instead. We learn to cope with fear so that it will be replaced with courage and confidence. We treat our sadness realistically as a part of the process of feeling optimism in the place of sadness. In each case we work toward the positive by recognition of the negative, dealing with it in such a way that it is replaced by the positive.

What about this idea that all we need to do is to think positive thoughts for our lives to emerge healthy, happy, and successful? Definitely, there is something to it! If parents try to think positive thoughts, emphasize the more satisfying emotions, and engage in positive speech and positive action, the atmosphere of the home will be improved. This is an ideal, of course, but ideals are valuable. We can aim toward them and keep getting closer to them. Having the ideal causes us to search for methods of coming constantly closer to these worthwhile goals.

MRS. WALLACE: Part of my religion is what you're talking about. I'm glad we have a pastor who emphasizes this ideal and he is a walking example, too. I've visited churches where the preacher sounded as if he was mad or the basis for what he said was fear. I don't like that.

Positive Living and Thinking

DR. CHEAVENS: A good many of the books written along these lines are written in the context of religion. One of the best known is *The Power of Positive Thinking*, written by a prominent Protestant minister, Dr. Norman Vincent Peale.[1] This remarkable book has sold several million copies.

Many professionals have branded this book as being superficial, but what we have to remember is that millions of people have been conditioned in Dr. Peale's brand of religion. Dr. Peale has extracted the positive elements of their belief for practice. His emphasis on the good results of thinking and repeating positive sayings certainly has experimental backing. All the "New Thought" religions or denominations lay heavy emphasis on thinking positive, happy thoughts. And there are a large number of individual pastors representing almost the entire spectrum of denominations who have the same emphasis. Many people have found what they need in these church groups. One very popular and readable book coming out of one of the new thought schools has sold about a million and a half copies—*In Tune with the Infinite*.[2] It's not always logical but has many helpful ideas.

From the Roman Catholic context, two books by one author, Ernest Dimnet, have a great deal of this emphasis—*The Art of Thinking* and *What We Live By*.[3]

Written by a Jewish rabbi, Joshua Liebman, *Peace of Mind*[4] has been widely read and a help to many people.

I would recommend reading any of these books or others that are somewhat similar which may appeal to you, because out of each of them will come at least a few very practical, usable ideas that may help you keep yourselves in a happy frame of mind.

Some of these books have been criticized as being superficial, and perhaps they are. Yet I am very slow to aim destructive criticism at books that have given so many people hope, confidence, and a generally higher morale.

Some of the books of this kind tend to overlook the question of what to do about negative emotions when they occur or when they are persistent. The release that comes from talking about worry, fear, anger, or sorrow is in itself a positive thing, clearing the way for more positive emotions and thoughts. The constructive channeling of the energy that comes from fear and anger can become a positive force when these emotions occur.

I know that people can change their own lives so that they experience more of the happy emotions, have more happy thoughts, and more satisfying activities. So when we say "accept" a negative emotion, it does not mean that we think this emotion is desirable. We just mean we understand that it is natural, just like the hiccups, or tiredness. We don't feel that anger at the members of one's own family is a crime. Neither is fear something to be ashamed of and hidden. They are natural reactions and the only important question is what to do about them for our own good and the good of others.

It might be well to say that sadness and depression, particularly if they are fairly superficial, can be counteracted by some stimulating, pleasant activity. Since the bodily processes are retarded during depression, some physical activity that stimulates the circulation would certainly be helpful. But any sort of distracting and pleasant activity might do the trick. This strategy of distraction also may work effectively with both fear and anger.

Anger Caused by a Lack of Skill

Another point for parents to remember is that a great deal of the anger of children is caused by their lack of skill. The child wishes to reach a goal but when he begins to work toward it, he finds that the necessary skills for its achievement are not developed. So the child is frustrated and becomes angry. Or he may be disappointed and become depressed.

As the child grows older, he gradually acquires all sorts of skills that will help him reach his goals. Experimentally, it has been discovered that children with certain skills have less anger and are less destructive than children who did not have these skills. Parents must be patient in this area, but also see to it that the children have opportunities to develop all sorts of skills. As they do, the occasions for anger and depression due to this type of frustration grow less and less.

Pleasurable Emotions

We have talked about fear, anger, and sadness. We have not discussed fully the emotions connected with pleasure. Physiologically, the body during pleasure is subject to less tension, digestion is better, circulation is good, and the entire organism works more efficiently.

Perhaps the major source of the pleasurable emotions is from satisfying relations with other people. This may be from mother or father, brothers or sisters, relatives or friends. These satisfying emotions have their basis in the close affectionate relationship of the infant with the mother. The scope of affection is quickly broadened to include the father and other members of the family.

As we have said before, the period of fetal development is important to these good human relations. If the mother is happy about her pregnancy, and if she remains generally happy throughout pregnancy, apparently the baby has a better chance for later healthful emotional development.

As the infant develops, pleasure is derived not only from the affections of the family, but from play and various other activities. And, as the child develops, achievement brings pleasure, particularly the achievements that are creative. Learning motivated by curiosity, the wish to find out about things, brings pleasure. New experiences also bring their own satisfactions.

MRS. VICTOR: I suppose one of the reasons I enjoyed our discussions on creativity was because I get so much pleasure out of creative activity.

MR. VICTOR: She has recently gotten a sizable price for one of her paintings. I'm about ready to retire and let her make the living!

MRS. VICTOR: And the children get so much fun out of their creative activities, too.

DR. CHEAVENS: Thanks for bringing this out, because creative activity is one of the big reasons for happy living.

Even with the pleasurable emotions, we parents sometimes cramp our children's style. The children become noisy because the game they are playing is exhilarating. We say, "You're making too much noise. Quiet down!" Noise, loud laughter, shouting, and yelling may all be natural expressions of joy. What is wrong with us parents that a little noise gets on our nerves so much?

Or the child is laughing and we say, "Don't laugh so loud." Maybe he needs to laugh loud as a release.

Think of all the no's and don'ts we give the children about all their emotional expressions. We say, "Don't cry," when perhaps crying is needed. Wouldn't it be better to say, "You're hurt—it will stop in a minute," or, "You're disappointed."

We say, "You mustn't be angry." Wouldn't it be better to say, "That makes you mad. Don't you want to tell me about it?" Or we say, "Don't be afraid." Why not "Of course you're afraid. Tell me just how you feel. Everybody gets afraid sometimes."

So we end up saying to ourselves, "Let's be more accepting and more understanding of our children's emotions. Let's allow our children freer expression of all their emotions." And if this makes us feel unsure of ourselves and afraid that things will get out of hand, let us remember that children can learn to direct all their emotional expressions constructively. The child is teachable in this area just as in all the other areas of his life. And above all, let us foster their creative activities.

FOOTNOTES

1. Norman Vincent Peale, *The Power of Positive Thinking* (New York: Fawcett World Library, 1965).

2. Ralph Waldo Trine, *In Tune with the Infinite* (New York: The Bobbs-Merrill Company, 1947).

3. Ernest Dimnet, *The Art of Thinking* (New York: Simon and Schuster, 1928). *What We Live By* (New York: Simon and Schuster, 1932).

4. Joshua Loth Liebman, *Peace of Mind* (New York: Simon and Schuster, 1946).

17. The Advantage of Well-Balanced Sex Education

DR. CHEAVENS: In your requests for us to discuss certain topics as we began these meetings, a number were nearly unanimous choices. One of these was the very ticklish and controversial business of the child's sex education.

There are two areas of life around which there are probably more personality disturbances than all the other areas put together. One of these has previously been discussed—the area of hostility, and particularly toward the members of one's own family. The other is that of sex, although I hesitate to put it in a compartment by itself. In real life it is not compartmentalized at all. The child sees sex behavior as he observes animal life. He sees affectionate behavior on the part of his parents. And he sees sex, and not always in the best light, at the theater or on T.V. Nevertheless one's attitudes toward sex and one's own sex behavior sometimes may be the sources of considerable difficulty.

Affectionate Ties Are the Foundation

The relation of each child to his parents and their relationship to him are crucial. If love and understanding and companionship exist, the child is well on his way to establishing a good foundation for later sex relations. This sort of thing we're not afraid to talk about. It is the sex information area which most parents are afraid of. Let me say that this area is largely a mechanical one and really isn't hard to learn. And it is important for the child to get accurate information.

154

MRS. ZIMMER: Don't you think our early upbringing is mostly responsible for this. In my family, sex was not branded as bad. Almost everything about it was just a tabu subject. So the children, and there were three of us, just inferred it was bad. Well, a good example of this is that many people referred to a woman's undergarments as "unmentionables" (laughter erupted from the group).

DR. CHEAVENS: I think you're right and a good many of us went through the same experience. Many parents felt it was their duty to inform the children and did so. But it turned out to be a strained, embarrassed sort of one-way talk, the sooner over the better. You might even call it "instant" sex information, which was really little better than nothing.

As I said, very likely the foundation for a wholesome sex life lies in the affectionate ties between young children and their parents, in the relationships of sisters and brothers in the family, and perhaps later in the relation of the child to his playmates. Satisfying social relationships are certainly an important part of the prelude to satisfying heterosexual relations in adulthood. It is this positive side of one's early social relations that needs every opportunity to develop.

An abundance of affection in the family usually means that the young child forms the basis for good relationships outside the family. And these good friendships are all an essential part of personality development that will later contribute to a satisfying marital relationship, including the overtly sexual side of this relationship.

However, the average parent worries about a good many small and sometimes trivial matters that relate to sex. And these trivial matters, if not looked at in a constructive way, and if handled unwisely, may become anything but trivial later.

Curiosity About Sex Is Normal

Although there are a good many individual differences between children, generally our children begin to develop interest in their own bodies at about six months of age. This increases until the child is about a year of age. It is part of the child's normal development (according to Dr. Gesell, between 40 and 52 weeks of age) to explore every part of his body, including the genitals.[1] Beginning at about six months the infant's ability to use his hands to explore his world is increased rapidly, and his body is an important part of that world.

Most children outgrow the manual manipulation of their genital organs rather quickly. Again this will vary from child to child. The average child under Gesell's observation handled the sex organs at thirty months of age when clothes were removed. If parents are overconcerned when this normal exploration is taking place, if they express horror, shock, excitement, or if the child is punished, the infantile exploration may become prolonged and excessive.

If parents find themselves tense when they observe the infant engaging in this normal exploration, to relieve parental tension the parent should have a toy handy and put this into the infant's hands. This is partly to pacify parents who find themselves fearful and insecure when observing the baby handling his sex organs. Nevertheless, it is a good strategy.

Again, about the worst thing that can be done is to express shock and revulsion verbally or otherwise to punish the baby with slapping or other such measures. All of this simply makes matters worse. But this attitude and behavior has been rather common.

Naturally, it is good commonsense to have enough toys within reach of the baby so he can satisfy his normal drive to reach with his hands, to explore and handle objects in his environment. And with interesting objects within reach, the child will not resort to handling the various parts of his body as much as he would without such objects.

Many authorities feel that by five years of age the child should have outgrown infantile handling of sex organs. Many, of course, outgrow it earlier. Most children also learn what behavior is acceptable in public, or only in the home, and what behavior the culture forces them to engage in privately. If there is excessive handling of sex organs, the first step is to consult the pediatrician, who would be able to determine whether there is some physical cause such as an irritation. The pediatrician would also help in finding probable psychological causes, such as lack of affection.

At any rate, it is reassuring to the parent to find out that this handling of the sex organs is normal behavior for the infant, and equally reassuring to know that it is usually outgrown by age five. The less tense, the less alarmed, the less angry parents become because of this normal behavior, the less prone the child will be to prolong it.

Learning Can Be Casual

Part of the sex education of the young child is learning the differences between male and female. This can be achieved so casually, so normally, that excessive preoccupation with matters of sex can be avoided. In families where there are boys and girls, letting the children undress together, or a policy of no locked doors during bathtime, results in the child's accepting these sex differences as routinely as they accept the sex differences in the animals they observe.

With the only child, many parents find that the observation of sex differences in animals may certainly help, but will not completely satisfy the child's curiosity. Pictures are a big help and usually there is available statuary that may also be of help.

MRS. KASTLY: I have been the mother of an only child. Melba will soon be three and is very advanced for her age. This only-child condition will be over in about two months, as you can easily see, if things continue to go well. But what you said about looking at pictures has been successful. An older book, but still very good, is Frances Strain's *New Patterns in Sex Teaching*.[2] One picture in the book is of a very well-done bronze statuary named *Boy with a Fish* that has been informing for Melba. Also, I have a friend with a baby boy about a year old. Melba has watched the bathing of this child a good many times. She enjoys helping give the baby a bath. Looking at the nude boy has just become a natural and casual affair.

Take a Positive Attitude

DR. CHEAVENS: From Mrs. Kastly's account we can see how simple it is. Noticing the difference between male and female nevertheless may cause some concern for both parent and child. Usually the child's concern will express itself in questions. The matter-of-fact, calm answer to these questions as a rule takes care of the concern. Most authorities agree that a child has less concern over sexual differences if they are observed in children their own age or younger. More concern is generated by the nudity of adults. However, if the child happens to observe the nudity of adults, again there should not be shock, shame, or horror expressed—nor anger because the child has burst into the bedroom or bathroom. These disturbed parental emotions connected with nudity only serve to create more tension about sex differences.

Children's questions should be accurately answered, giving sex organs or any part of the body the proper name. It is hoped that the parent can do this without embarrassment. But so many parents have grown up under circumstances that make for embarrassment about sex that this may be hoping too much. Even if the parent feels embarrassment, he should go ahead and answer the questions accurately when they are asked. This may help the parent to be less embarrassed later when other similar questions arise.

It is to be expected that with a number of children experiences of sex-play will take place. These may be of various kinds, such as a mutual undressing and exposure or fondling. Again the worst that can come out of this is for the adults to express horror or anger, or punish the children harshly. It seems that the most desirable attitude toward these sometimes unavoidable experiences should be about the same as when children throw food across the table. This is not in good taste. It just "isn't done." This attitude puts the whole matter on the basis of our accepted standards of behavior, and not on the basis of some terrible crime which has been committed.

The guilt feelings that grow in the child when adults show horror or anger, or when they shame the child excessively, or punish him, merely mean that sex becomes more of a problem to this child who sees the whole thing pictured as ugly, undesirable, or even nasty and repulsive.

When children ask questions and are given accurate, straightforward answers, they may still not understand. But one thing they do understand is that the parent is trying to help them. Later they may return with the same question. Lines of communication are established and are kept open.

Sex Education Is a Continuing Process

This means, of course, that sex education is, and should be, a continuing process. The parent certainly should not rush things. This, in its way, may be almost as undesirable as not enough information. If the lines of communication are kept open, the child will nearly always ask questions as he feels a need to have them answered. The questions provide easy cues for the parents.

If questions are not forthcoming at the age when a parent expects them (and there are many individual differences here) then a book which is discussed frankly or a conversation about the breeding and reproduction of animals may open the lines of communication.

As a continuing program, the role of the school in sex education becomes important. Through the study of science, particularly biology, the broad aspects of mating and reproduction become an integrated part of the curriculum.

In the primary grades it may be done in various ways. Hamsters, with all their cunning ways and their wonderful fertility, have been the subjects of observation of many primary age children all over the country. In the open discussion of mating and reproduction, boys and girls talk about these matters as they should, as a normal part of the life processes.

Some states have been much more advanced than others in providing the materials for these discussions, although even in these more advanced states, some communities are woefully backward. In the schools where sex education is integrated with health, biology, or social studies, as a natural part of the curriculum, boys and girls accept it as normally as they should, and discuss it as objectively as any of the other biological functions of living creatures.

In summing up, let us emphasize two points. The first of these is to repeat that the loved, accepted child has one of the most important parts of the foundation for a happy sex life later. A wholesome social development is an essential prelude to later satisfying social relationships, of which sex is a part.

The second point is that each child should have such varied opportunities to develop his creativity, that he will have absorbing creative interests as long as he lives. This we discussed fully when we discussed creativity. It is rather well agreed that creative outlets help the child in many ways. Among these, satisfying creative activities help to keep sex expression in proper perspective. The child who is well-developed socially, and who has ample creative activities, will tend also to have a more satisfying sex life.

FOOTNOTES

1. Arnold Gesell and F. L. Ilg, *Infant and Child in the Culture Today* (New York: Harper & Bros., 1943), p. 336.
2. Frances B. Strain, *New Patterns in Sex Teaching* (New York: Appleton-Century-Crofts, 1951).

18. Advantages of
Handling Problems in a Positive Way

DR. CHEAVENS: We have selected this session to discuss specific problems—a discussion which could go on indefinitely since there are more than a score of problems we could touch on. However, I have taken several that the group indicated as being of special interest to them. Also I have taken the liberty of selecting several of our number to present the topics. They have read in good authorities, but we shall still have each topic open for further discussion. We shall first have Mr. Victor's topic: Thumb-sucking.

Thumb-sucking

MR. VICTOR: Thumb-sucking seems to be widespread among infants in our country and in European countries. In fact, some of the studies indicate that about half of the babies investigated go through a period of thumb- or finger-sucking. A great majority of parents worry about this habit. Many feel that it is a symptom of personality disturbance.

This may be true only in a few cases. The child who keeps on sucking the thumb past school age may have rather serious feelings of insecurity, or in some cases it may be a symptom of immaturity. It would be a mistake to diagnose all late thumb-suckers, however, as having serious disturbances. Each one is an individual and the symptom of thumb-sucking should be considered in the light of the child's total personality. Since most parents worry especially about the late thumb-sucker it would be well to consult expert professional medical help as to the meaning of the symptom and what could be done about it.

But let's consider the symptom in babies. Usually it occurs when the child is hungry, tired, or sleepy. A good substitute for thumb or fingers is the pacifier. Many authorities agree that the habit of sucking a pacifier is not so hard to break as thumb- or finger-sucking. However, Dr. Gesell of Yale, who has studied behavior patterns such as this in very large numbers of children, reports that thumb-sucking reaches its peak in most children who practice it, between eighteen and twenty-one months.[1] By the time most of these children are three years of age, the habit begins to weaken. Most three-year-olds who fall asleep sucking the thumb will allow it to be removed when they are asleep. By the time the majority of children are five they will cooperate with parents in almost any reasonable plan designed to help them drop the habit. This was true of our youngest. When he was four we had several periods of talking about it, and he quit of his own accord.

DR. CHEAVENS: What Dr. Gesell has done, of course, is to establish statistical averages. If a child follows or is better than the average, the parent is reassured. But if the child is worse than the average, the parent sometimes begins to worry. Again we need to remember that children are individuals and it is very unlikely that any of them will conform to averages. In order to establish an average some will be better and some worse. The average rarely hits the individual.

MRS. WALLACE: When I read Dr. Gesell, I worried because Mary still sucked her thumb when she was five. But as I grew less tense about it and had a more positive attitude, the thumb-sucking began to disappear and in a few months was gone.

MR. WALLACE: She was worried about Mary's teeth. I water-ski with a dentist who told me that the shape of the baby teeth is not too important. That helped.

MR. VICTOR: I think this generally about covers the topic except to say that most children drop thumb- and finger-sucking by school age. If the school child persists in the habit, some teachers are skilled in helping to break it. In school, hands stay rather busy, anyway, doing many interesting things. Also, the other children may tease the thumb-sucker, who will usually abandon the behavior in self-defense.

Parents also worry about the damage that may be done to the child's teeth as Mr. Wallace has said. While the structure of baby teeth is sometimes changed, most authorities agree that the permanent teeth will not be affected if the child has lost the habit by the time the permanent teeth come in.

MRS. ZIMMER: I worried a lot about Jane who kept on sucking

her thumb until she was almost six. My doctor suggested that, while it wasn't really best, I should apply that hot stuff to her thumb, if I was going to keep on worrying. Well, I did, but I explained to Jane *why* I was doing it. She had already said she did it absent-mindedly and wasn't conscious of it. So I told her that the hot stuff would remind her and make her conscious of it. In about three days it was all over. But I don't claim that this is best. Really I didn't know how to stop worrying about it.

Dr. CHEAVENS: Perhaps your explanation and reasoning undid any particular harm in the method.

Mrs. Sonneman has made a special study of bed-wetting, and I have asked her to bring a brief summary of her findings.

Bed-wetting

Mrs. SONNEMAN: The technical name for bed-wetting is enuresis, and it is usually applied to a four- or five-year-old or older who still wets the bed. The time of developing this nighttime bladder control will vary from child to child. The parent should not be too disturbed if a child is a bit late in learning to sleep dry.

Some studies indicate that a large percentage of children begin to sleep dry at two years of age. However, Gesell says that some three-year-olds sleep dry throughout the night and some awaken by themselves and ask to be taken to the toilet. The four-year-old does better, with lapses when he is about to be ill or when the weather is turning colder. The average five-year-old shows still more improvement, with fewer lapses. Even the school-age child may have occasional accidents due to a number of different causes.[2]

Some authorities give a diagnosis of enuresis if a child habitually wets the bed after age three. It seems that this is expecting too much of the average three-year-old, although intelligent and affectionate teaching (with no punishment for failure) should certainly be employed to help the three-year-old who still has not learned control.

There are a number of theories about possible psychological causes of enuresis. Let's look at the ones we hear most commonly. One is that the child is immature for his age. Another is that the child is emotionally disturbed, either due to excitement, tension, or anxiety. Still another theory says that the bed-wetting is a bid for attention and an attempt to get more help from parents. Other theorists hold that the child is unconsciously showing hostility toward his parents.

There may be something to some or all of these theories. In some cases more than one of these causes might combine to produce the trouble. There is abundant evidence that psychological difficulties are sometimes factors in causing enuresis.

However, within the past ten years, there are some reliable studies that may help both physicians and parents understand the problem better, and deal with it more effectively. One investigation studied over 80 bed-wetting children, comparing them with over 800 children who were not bed-wetters. They found no significant differences between the emotional adjustment of the two groups.[3]

Another interesting study was published the same year as the one above. This investigator found a high incidence of restricted bladder capacity among enuretic children.[4] Here, then, is a physical reason.

From the first of these two reports we have indications that emotional disturbances may not loom quite as large as has sometimes been thought as causes of enuresis. And from the second study we are led to feel that physical causes may loom larger than many had thought. Yet in neither case should we too hastily jump at conclusions, because there is other evidence.

For example, one able group of investigators found that mothers who had the greatest anxiety about sex, who showed little affection toward the child and were severe in toilet training had children who continued to prolong bed-wetting. Parents who were less severe and more affectionate toward the children were found to have fewer children who were bed-wetters.[5]

Conditioning procedures have been used as remedies. One method that is now considered too disturbing is a mechanical device which automatically administers an electric shock to a child when he wets the bed. It is reported that disturbed children become more disturbed when this method is used.[6]

Several teams of investigators have used a pad electrically constructed to set off a bell when the first few drops of urine strike a pad. This is not a severe training method and has been fairly successful.[7]

Another team increased the intake of liquids during the day to expand the capacity of the bladder. They encouraged the children to postpone urinating as long as possible. Thirty children treated with this method were all cured, which is most encouraging. This is a very practical measure that the average parent might try, but it is still not well established.

In some cases the child-guidance center might be of assistance. Here the child will usually go through a course of play-therapy, and is helped with his emotional problems, and conferences are also held with parents.

Some children are prone to regressive bed-wetting. When a baby is born and the older child feels neglected, even though he has previously been sleeping dry, he may return to bed-wetting. This is thought to be a bid for attention, or affection and companionship from parents. Whatever the cause, or causes, the affection of the parent is needed and if the child is given affectionate help, he will usually begin to sleep dry again soon.

MR. SHELBY: I would like to give my own experience which, of course, might not apply to others. When Jake was five he was still wetting the bed. So I talked to our pediatrician. He told me that we would work on it and he was almost sure we could use a method that was successful. He said first he wanted me to try something that had been good during World War II. The army had a group of men that were still bed-wetters. They put them in a barracks together and mainly used one method. They rewarded success and ignored failure. For months they did this and cured most of the men. So he told me to try it with Jake.

MRS. KASTLY: But suppose Jake didn't have any successes— that he wet the bed every night? Then what would you do?

MR. SHELBY: This was taken care of. When we took Jake up at about eleven or twelve at night, I was to compliment him on sleeping dry that long and encourage him not to wet during the rest of the night. Granted he was at least half-asleep. The doctor said he would understand, anyway. So I did it. And it worked. Harold, the eight-year-old, sleeps with Jake. He became a wonderful rewarder. He complimented Jake all over the place and there was a good reason. (Laughter.) But anyway, it worked. I rewarded success and ignored failure. Incidentally, this has helped me in a lot of other things about what the boys do. But it stopped the bed-wetting!

DR. CHEAVENS: This is a most interesting example. Our next discussion is on the topic of stuttering, led by Mrs. Lovelace.

Stuttering

MRS. LOVELACE: If your child stutters there is definitely something you can do that will help. A good medical examination would come first. In some cases there may be physical causes for this disorder.

Incidentally there are close to two million—I think around

1,800,000—stutterers in the United States alone, and the disorder is distributed all over the world.

There have been a number of theories for the cause of stuttering, but one seems to be most in favor today and to a great many parents it sounds like commonsense. This is that stuttering is caused by something in a child's life that makes him very tense about the process of speech. Many times parents are hypercritical, so the child begins talking under a handicap. One of the leading authorities today is Dr. Wendell Johnson, Professor of Speech Pathology at the University of Iowa. Dr. Johnson conducted a careful study of a sizable number of stutterers compared with a similar number of nonstutterers. [8]

There were very few differences in the two groups except stuttering. But there was one chief difference between the parents of stutterers and the parents of nonstutterers. Parents of the speech-problem children had been much more tense about the imperfections of their children's speech almost from the beginning. That is, these parents worried about the very normal repetitions of sounds and words that occur in nearly all children as they learn to speak.

Therapy consisted in "a type of counseling of parents designed to get them to regard their children as normal, to give major attention . . . to the conditions affecting the youngster's speech." In general, parents were taught to reduce the tensions of the home and to be less demanding of their children in regard to both speech and their general behavior, and to make it easier for the stuttering child to gain approval and have feelings of success.

With this type of counseling 85 percent of the children improved in a short time and over 70 percent became normal in speech. So the outlook is encouraging if your child has this speech problem.

However, a word of caution should be added. If your child stutters, you should seek the best professional help and the earlier the better.

MRS. PUTNAM: I'm very lucky, I suppose, but none of my large brood of boys has developed any speech troubles. But don't most stutterers just outgrow the difficulty, anyway?

MRS. LOVELACE: I would say the reason for your boys' not having speech difficulties is your very flexible and relaxed attitude toward them. My reading has shown that very few children outgrow their speech difficulty. They need good help and so do their parents.

Almost anything in the home creating excess tension might be a partial cause of this speech disturbance. In one case with which I am acquainted, at about age three the younger of two brothers began to stutter. The mother became worried and this made the situation worse. The older brother (three years older) was an unusually able, very calm, cooperative youngster. The younger brother was headstrong and impulsive.

Through counseling, the mother came to see that it was the inability of the younger boy to compete with the older that was creating most of the problem. She began a program of easing the competition and seeing to it that the younger succeeded more and was in fewer situations where the comparison with his brother would throw him in an unfavorable light. Also the mother became less tense. After a few months of this program, stuttering disappeared.

Most of the authorities seem to agree on the need for changes to be brought about in the child's environment, and most important the social environment. The parents are usually the strongest forces in the social environment, although brothers and sisters might also be important. With older children, skilled counseling has many times proven helpful and, in certain cases, so has group therapy.

MR. INMAN: Aren't there other speech problems besides stuttering?

MRS. LOVELACE: I'm sorry, but I got my material on stuttering only. I know there are other problems. Maybe Dr. Cheavens will give you what you want.

Other Speech Defects

DR. CHEAVENS: Delayed speech refers to either a failure to talk or a retention of infantile patterns of speech. The major cause in most cases is mental retardation. However, there are many other causes, such as deafness, paralysis, or prolonged illness. Lack of motivation is sometimes indicated, as are also emotional conflict and aphasia. Since most of these causes are related to medical diagnosis, the services of a competent physician and perhaps later a speech therapist would be indicated.

By far the greatest number of speech defects are those involving problems of articulation. Examples of this are the substitution of one letter for another or omitting, slighting, or distorting letter sounds. A word of encouragement here is that from the first through fourth grades these troubles with articulation usually tend to grow less. But the advice of a good speech therapist would certainly be called for.

Our last topic on which Mrs. Zimmer will speak is temper tantrums.

Temper Tantrums

MRS. ZIMMER: In the discussion of emotions, the appropriate and constructive expression of anger and aggression was brought out. The temper tantrum is neither appropriate nor constructive. It usually occurs in the child of three years of age or under, and shows itself by uncontrolled expression of anger such as crying, screaming, falling on the floor, kicking, head-bumping, or fist-pounding.

Fortunately as most children grow older they tend to have fewer temper tantrums. In any case the temper tantrum has a cause or causes, and knowing these is an important part of solving the problem.

Generally speaking, the cause is frustration of some kind. The child is thwarted in some goal he is striving toward, this angers him, and his anger gets out of control.

Punishing the temper tantrum may stop the actual behavior, but nearly always the parent can make sure it increases the emotion of anger, and so punishment really defeats itself. Working intelligently to eliminate causes is much more effective.

Some parents are very inconsiderate of their children, roughly interrupting play or some other interesting activity which could be continued until some more logical time when a pause occurs. The parent could say, "When you finish this, will you please come on to dinner" (or whatever the child needs to do). This sort of considerate respect for the child's feelings pays big dividends in enlisting cooperation and preventing undue anger.

Parents should examine their own attitudes toward the child to determine if the child is being mistreated in any way, or neglected. A parental change of attitude, with more affectionate companionship given the child and a striving for fair, considerate treatment, will many times result in preventing the temper tantrums.

As suggested in the chapter on emotion, very young children grow frustrated because of their own lack of skill in achieving their goals. As skill increases there is less frustration.

Behind all or nearly all temper tantrums lies frustration, as we mentioned. There may be too many frustrations in your child's environment. If this is the case, you can help by reducing the number and sometimes the kinds of frustration he must meet. But it would certainly be unrealistic to attempt to remove all frustration from his life. Every child must learn to live with a certain amount of frustration and tolerate it. This is a normal and apparently a necessary part of the maturing process.

So you can show your child that his parents don't and can't have everything they want. You can show him that this is also true of other children, and that he must learn to put up with it.

Neither is it good to grant all your child's wishes, even those that can be granted, right away. Delay in getting what we want is another frustration we must all learn to tolerate. And most of the time we must learn to work for what we want and that involves delay.

When the temper tantrum occurs, the child should never gain his wish because of it. This leads to a repetition of the device because he knows it will gain his ends. It becomes a useful tool to him.

One of those ends may be to cause you concern. So don't show worry or fear or anger at his uncontrolled kicking, head-banging, and screaming. Walk off and leave the child and the temper tantrum. Without an audience it will soon subside.

If the cause of it is fundamental and you are at fault, correct the fault. If your child needs more affection and companionship, give him what he needs. If he is in a constantly frustrating situation, see to it that he is relieved. Put him into situations where he can succeed.

Even if a child has no temper tantrums, constant frustration is defeating and depressing. Sometimes a child is placed beyond his present capabilities in school and is subjected to frustrations beyond the point of tolerance. The guiding principle is to give the child tasks at which he can succeed and gradually increase the difficulty of these tasks.

DR. CHEAVENS: All of this has been good coverage on each problem. We can say that with all these specific problems there are some guiding principles. There must always be an abundance of affection. An attitude of confidence that the problem can and will be solved is a productive attitude for the parent and is contagious, so that the child also begins to feel confident that he can solve his own problems.

A flexible attitude is always conducive to better problem-solving. Perhaps grandmother and great grandmother and even so modern a person as mother advocated solving all the problems by the painful application of switch or hairbrush. This is a very rigid, stereotyped approach to solving problems, no matter who advocates it.

The intelligent approach is that the parent can, with searching and considerable thought, find the best solution to any problem. No two children are alike and no two problems are exactly alike. But all problems have solutions. With confidence and with intelligent research, solutions will be forthcoming. If the problem is a serious one, expert help is nearly always available.

On our next topic having to do with mental and emotional health related to religious faith, the consensus of the group was for me to discuss this. I am perfectly willing to, for I consider it a most important subject. However, if you have questions or points of view that need voicing, I want you to feel free to bring them.

FOOTNOTES

1. Arnold Gesell and Frances Ilg, *Infant and Child in the Culture of Today* (New York: Harper & Bros. 1943), pp. 306–307.

2. Ibid., pp. 331–32.

3. F. Tapia, et al., "Enuresis, an emotional symptom," *Journal of Nervous and Mental Disease* 130 (1960), 61–66.

4. S. R. Muellner, "Development of Urinary control in children: some aspects of the cause and treatment of primary enuresis," *Journal of the American Medical Association* 172 (1960), 1256–61.

5. R. R. Sears, et al., *Patterns of Child-Rearing* (Evanston, Ill.: Row, Peterson and Co., 1957), p. 131. See also B. R. McCandless, *Children and Adolescents* (New York: Holt, Rinehart, and Winston, 1961), pp. 87–91.

6. Muellner, op. cit.

7. James C. Coleman, *Abnormal Psychology and Modern Life*, 3rd ed. (Chicago: Scott, Foresman, 1964), pp. 358–59.

8. Wendell Johnson, *Stuttering* (Minneapolis: University of Minnesota Press, 1956), pp. 37–73.

19. Advantages to Mental Health of a Vital Religious Faith

DR. CHEAVENS: While you have kindly asked me to make a lecture of this, I am still going to open the question to discussion from time to time, since the very topic stimulates different points of view.

With the prediction that one person in every ten will at some time in his life be hospitalized for serious mental illness, you are eager to provide the home environment that will be most conducive to mental health for your child. More and more of the authorities in this field are seeing the need for a vital and rational religious faith as an important factor contributing to mental health.

A few years ago a well-known psychologist, Dr. Henry C. Link, wrote a significant book entitled *The Return to Religion*. In his work as special advisor for the Adjustment Service of New York City, Dr. Link made an analysis of some ten thousand cases who had used the Service. The evaluation was made on the basis of comprehensive case histories and the results of a very large battery of psychological tests. One of the results of this study was the finding that people who "believed in religion or attended church had significantly better personalities than those who did not." [1]

Reinforcing the results of his statistical study were the hundreds of people whom he interviewed personally. Among these he found that the practice of religion helped people solve their personal problems, make up their personal deficiencies, gave them a feeling of security, and in many similar ways was helpful to them.

Dr. Link was far from being the first person to observe these positive effects of vital religion upon those who practiced it. Dr. Link's people who practiced their religion had better personalities.

This is a desirable goal and doubtless includes many of the factors in personality which keep the individual well-balanced emotionally, mentally and socially.

But Dr. Carl G. Jung, one of the three great pioneers who explored the dynamics of human personality, goes deeper and further in stating the role of religion. After many decades of treating disturbed people, from the neurotic to the severely psychotic, Dr. Jung affirmed that, among all his patients over thirty-five years of age, without exception the central problem of them all was that of finding a "religious outlook on life." [2] These people, he said, had fallen ill because they had lost what living religion has to offer, and none of them was healed without regaining his religious outlook. He was talking about inner religion and not merely the outward signs of organized religion.

Mrs. Sonneman: Isn't Jung pretty much in disrepute today? I myself have found him very stimulating.

Dr. Cheavens: Jung's star is waning as you suggest, and yet he was one of the most brilliant and learned men of his day. You have said that you've found him stimulating. If more people would read him seriously perhaps he would have for them some message, also.

Both Link and Jung, though approaching human beings along different avenues, are saying that as your child matures, his chances for balance of personality and for mental health are better if he has a vital religious faith.

More recently another voice with convincing testimony has been heard. Dr. Arthur Cain is a clinical psychologist who treated thirty-nine alcoholics considered to be virtually hopeless cases.[3] Out of these, thirty-six recovered. Dr. Cain's therapy approaches the problems of personality disturbance from many angles. Each person (called a colleague) spends two hours a week in a counseling session. He devotes time to constructive and relevant reading, and he also keeps a diary of his thoughts and actions. He is given vocational guidance. He participates each week in the activities of some social organization of his own choosing. There is also the development of aesthetic appreciation.

Each person under therapy participates in "religious investigation." Commenting on this, Dr. Cain writes that he himself had been an avowed agnostic since youth. But much of the conversation with his patients in regard to religion involved vocabulary and concepts which were unfamiliar to Dr. Cain. So he enrolled in a course in religion at Columbia University. He was amazed at the way in which the professor fused "three apparently incompatible

disciplines—psychology, religion, and philosophy," and he began
to understand that the three disciplines were not at all incompatible.

Each of the colleagues undertook with open mind to approach
the question of his own personal religion anew. So "religious recovery" became an essential part of the recovery from alcoholism.
Much of the recommended reading tied in with religion. Dr. Cain
sums it up by saying, "It was the reading of certain books that
prepared the colleagues for religious investigation, and it was
through religious investigation that they attained serenity."

MR. VICTOR: Isn't Arthur Cain the one who was so critical of
Alcoholics Anonymous? It seems to me his criticism wasn't completely justified.

DR. CHEAVENS: I quite agree. Alcoholics Anonymous has ac-
complished great good with a large number of people who otherwise might not have been helped. While Dr. Cain had a point in
his article in *Harper's* which was later reprinted in his book, my own
feeling toward A.A. is that they are due great credit. Their well-
known achievements are in part due to an emphasis on reliance on
a higher power to help the alcoholic free himself from addiction. It
would seem that for life to be balanced, personal religion is a necessity for most people.

Dr. David B. Klein, professor of psychology and director of
Psychological Services at the University of Southern California,
makes an acute observation in regard to one of the basic needs of
man. Even the person who is mature emotionally and mentally continues to have dependency needs. The infant's needs for safety and
protection are filled by the loving parent. "This provides the way
for the child's later religious orientation and the emergence of attitudes of reverence toward the concept of God as protective father,
guide, comforter and source of authority." [4]

Thus far in our discussion, the term "vital religious faith" has
been repeated. In the definition of this term, that approach to religion which exploits and increases fear I would omit. Such religion
is negative or, more accurately, destructive.

MR. SHELBY: Aren't many of our acknowledged leaders in religion the kind that appeal mainly to fear, or to anger, for their
results?

MRS. WALLACE: As all of you know, I am very loyal to my
church and my religion. They mean a great deal to me. I think they
are good for my children, too. This baby that will be here in about
three months will also be brought up with this attitude. But you
may make sure I got into a church that did not have the negative or
destructive approach.

MR. SHELBY: Well, I listened to a well-known evangelist the other day and it didn't take a brilliant mind to see that his appeal was to fear.

DR. CHEAVENS: Regrettably, there is much truth in what you're saying. But, there would be rather general agreement among the authorities on mental health that those religious teachings which magnify horror and emphasize punishment would be detrimental to mental health.

Those elements in religion which raise morale, increase confidence, inspire hope, and in general liberate the energies of the person for constructive achievement, are the elements which make for betterment in human conditions. And perhaps greatest of all is the ideal present in most religious teaching of satisfying and harmonious relations between people.

For such harmonious relationships the language of religion has a number of expressions—love, good-will, brotherhood, communion. Perhaps the most common is the word love. Without love, life is meaningless and empty. With it life is rich and full and significant.

Commenting on the necessity for love between people, the late Pitirim Sorokin, who was president of the American Sociological Association and a professor at Harvard, has much to say for what he calls "creative, unselfish love." [5]

He states that the "curative and integrating power of love" shows itself in many forms. If babies are to grow into mentally and morally sound individuals, love is indispensible. "Many sociological studies show that the bulk of juvenile delinquents are recruited from the children who in early life did not have the necessary minimum of love."

Sorokin names a long list of psychiatrists and psychologists who are authorities on psychotherapy, who agree that the chief "curative agent" in their various methods is "empathy, kindness, and mutual trust."

Sorokin sums up his discussion by stating that love "can pacify international conflicts," that it is "a life-giving force, necessary for physical, mental and moral health; altruistic persons live longer than egotistic individuals; love is a powerful antidote against criminal, morbid, and suicidal tendencies." He states that it is the religious institutions all over the world that have taught and exemplified love through the ages.

Likewise Alfred Adler, as has been pointed out in a previous chapter, who was frankly theistic, after dealing with multitudes of disturbed people came to the conclusion that egocentricity was the basis for much neurotic behavior.[6] The antidote was altruistic service, and there was a "universal law" taught in the scripture of religion, "Thou shalt love thy neighbor as thyself." A person not living in harmony with this law was inviting to himself disintegration and loss; the person living in accord with this law was attracting to himself integration and all the good of life.

Ashley Montagu, widely known anthropologist and author of many constructive books, states that the "essence of religious teachings is love" which "will always remain the supreme religious value." He goes on to say that scientific method has led man to the discovery that love is the main principle by which men must direct their lives and develop their values. Love leads man to work *with*, not against, his fellowman, and nature and the cosmos clearly "favor the cooperative." [7]

From the writing of this discerning scholar, we conclude that the manifestation of God in the life of man is largely through love. The teaching of both the Old and the New Testaments emphasizes that "God is Love."

MR. SHELBY: I am convinced my children should have a rational religion to make the most of their life. The question I find hardest to answer is how I as their father can best help them in achieving it.

MRS. DANA: Attitudes are contagious. If my attitude is one of faith, my children stand a good chance of having faith. My ideal is to keep my attitudes both intelligent and positive.

MRS. KASTLY: I think you're right. It's not so much what I tell my children to be. It's what I am day in and day out before them. They can sense that and they soak it up. They identify with their parents and this doesn't just mean imitation, which is important enough. They incorporate what we are into their thinking and feeling.

(A helpful discussion followed, in which almost all the group participated, about many different aspects of the subject of making religion practical in the home. Several members of the group were strong believers in secret prayer as a distinct help in solving problems of all kinds in the family. Nearly everyone agreed that the parents' example was of tremendous importance. Also, most of them were against being "preachy." They felt this would definitely turn the children away from some things that were very good. The entire group—as far as I could detect—were in favor of tolerance and flexibility in regard to religious belief and practice.)

DR. CHEAVENS: It is said that Ralph Waldo Emerson's mother went daily into her "secret place" of prayer and meditation. She did not talk about what transpired in that room. She did not have to. It was apparent in her bearing and in the expression of her face as she came out of her inner room, for each time she emerged, there was an unmistakable radiance to her face that bespoke that she was "in tune with the Infinite." Reading this, someone commented, "This helps explain the creative genius of Emerson, his devotion to the truth, and his dynamic faith."

That parent who daily exemplifies creative, unselfish love, who seeks to live the truth as he sees it, will be giving his child a daily contact with what might be called the God-process in human living. Of all that a parent can bestow upon his children, this is the supreme gift.

FOOTNOTES

1. Henry C. Link, *The Return to Religion* (New York: The Macmillan Company, 1936), p. 13.

2. Carl D. Jung, *Modern Man in Search of a Soul* (New York: Harcourt, Brace, 1933), p. 264.

3. Arthur H. Cain, *The Cured Alcoholic* (New York: The John Day Company, 1964), pp. 185–91.

4. David B. Klein, *Mental Hygiene* (New York: Henry Holt and Co., 1956), pp. 359–60.

5. Pitirim Sorokin, "The Powers of Creative Unselfish Love," in *New Knowledge in Human Values*, ed. Abraham Maslow (New York: Harper & Bros., 1959), pp. 7–12.

6. Phyllis Bottome, *Alfred Adler* (New York: The Vanguard Press, 1957), pp. 120–26.

7. M. F. Ashley Montagu, "This Is My Faith," in *This Is My Faith*, ed. Stewart G. Coles (New York: Harper & Bros., 1956), pp. 177–87.

20. You Can Give Your Child These Great Advantages

THE SERIES of discussions concluded with the problems brought out in the previous chapter. While there are other problems that are quite common, the group felt that the time had come to draw the meetings to a close. Each person was supplied with references to books that treated many other difficulties children might have. This concluding chapter sums up the essence of the learning of the group during its sessions.

The Bright Prospect of Good Choices

The outlook for parents who wish to provide the atmosphere most conducive to well-rounded, complete, optimal development for their children is exceedingly optimistic. Any child of given ability at birth, who has the right environment in which to mature, almost without exception will tend to approximate his fullest capacities.

Some years ago an experiment that has implications for humans was performed with chickens.[1] The biologist found out that chickens allowed to choose their own diets differed greatly in the foods they chose. They could be divided generally into two groups—the good choosers and the poor choosers. The good choosers grew larger and stronger and fended for themselves better in every way.

The investigator then fed the diet of the good choosers to the poor choosers and found that while the poor choosers improved, they never reached the level of development of the good choosers.

The major difference here as we apply this to human behavior is that people who are poor choosers can learn to be good choosers. You who have chosen to read this book are engaged in a search for better choices for yourself and your children. You are learning to be better choosers. Your search will be rewarded. As you inform yourself and as you experiment with possible better ways of living, you will gradually evolve a way of life that is superior to your old way of life.

It is also encouraging to know that your children can learn to be good choosers. As you set them the example they will be influenced in this direction. As you gradually allow them to exercise more and more choices, with the freedom to make mistakes, they can learn to make better and better choices. And most of the important issues of life depend upon the right choices people make.

This matter of good choices affects every area of life—choices of skills to be learned, choices in the social world, choices of marital partners, of creative vocations and avocations, of a moral code, and of a satisfying life-philosophy. In each of these life-territories the child can, through experience in a favorable atmosphere, learn to be a good chooser. And as he learns, he will choose not the inferior, not even the merely good, but the best.

The Strategic Position of the Parent

As a parent you are in an enviable position. You can create an environment in which your child will flourish. The mother *is* the environment of the unborn babe, with the father having much to do with his wife's well-being.

The mother can give her unborn child her own radiant health as she follows the available guidelines and chooses the best diet, the best exercise regimen, the best attitudes conducive to happy emotions, and the best available medical care.

After the birth of the baby you can continue to choose the environment for your child that will be best for him. His environment is made up chiefly of his parents. Your attitude of love, of confidence, of happiness will cause your child to blossom. The many affectionate contacts with you will be food for his developing personality. From the first he will begin to have a wholesome self-concept as he learns he is loved and cared for. Even this early he will begin to know he is a person of worth.

In the environment of affection with which you choose to surround your child will come the other elements the good-choosing parent can provide—the essential foods for a strong body, an enriched and stimulating environment in which he will have the freedom to respond and grow in intelligence and physical strength.

This environment of love, intellectual stimulation, and enrichment will continue in early childhood with opportunities to learn constantly present. In this flexible environment which opens doors to positive activities, your child will begin to acquire skills, slowly at first and then more rapidly. He will learn how to get along with other people, to give and to take, to get his rights and to give others their rights. In this atmosphere his curiosity will flourish and lead him into rewarding paths of learning.

Along with abundant affection, you will be able to provide your child the security of firmness in his world. There are things he can't do and you are firm on this. And there are things that have to be done. Here you are equally firm. He becomes a secure child in both your warmth for him and your firmness. In your firmness you are never harsh but couple firmness with affection.

In such an atmosphere of love and firmness, the child begins to care about living according to a sound code of conduct. It is this early *caring* about living according to a reasonable code that will give him the inner equipment as he matures to be a person who lives according to his own evolved ethical code.

In this atmosphere that you have chosen to create, your child's creativity will flourish. He will know the joys of creating and seeing his own individual original products take shape and become reality.

With an abundance of love your child will become a loving person, one who can give love and who can gratefully receive love.

As you demonstrate to him the intelligent channeling of your own emotions, he will learn to direct his anger constructively, to deal wisely with his fears, to throw off depression as it besets him. He will learn the quiet joy of living well, and his days will be interspersed with rapture. He will be possessed of confidence. High morale will lead him to self-realization and achievement.

The Environment Beyond the Home

As the child moves out from the home into greater fields of activities and social contacts, he will of course come under many influences. With the resilient personality he has developed in his home environment and from his learning to be a good chooser, the probability is very great that he will conduct himself with credit in all his confrontations.

But you as a parent have a certain amount of control on the environment beyond the home. Parents today who take an interest have much to do with shaping school policies. The same is true of other processes in the community. Concerned parents *can* reduce the amount of juvenile delinquency in their community. There are many ways for a parent to improve the community.

What we must work for in ourselves and in others is to get all parents to provide the best environment they can for the development of their children. This, as we have seen, takes a great deal of knowledge, and it requires a great deal of intelligently directed effort and work. It does not just happen.

The more parents who are gaining this knowledge and who are working to apply it, the better the chances of all children will be. In fact we still do not know what the child can become if he has the best atmosphere to grow up in. It is going to take many people working together to provide this kind of atmosphere. The more positive forces with which children are surrounded, the better their chances are. The fewer the forces that are negative for children in environment, the fewer the chances there are for them to develop poorly or in the wrong direction.

As long as your neighbor's children do not have their best chances for development, your own children's chances are cut down. Of course, there are limits to how much improvement you can bring for your neighbor's children. Commonsense dictates a great deal of what you can do. But there are goals toward which all of us can work in every community that will mean better chances for all children. Well-rounded programs of parent education is one of these. The best educational opportunities for all children is another goal toward which we can work.

It also goes beyond your own neighborhood and city. Almost every part of today's world is in fairly close touch with every other part. And communication is improving constantly. This means that what happens in Communist China and the Congo is of great importance to us here. For instance, what has been happening in Viet Nam definitely affects large numbers of people in the United States. This means that our goals for the betterment of mankind must be world-wide goals. Man can be improved physically, mentally, socially, and in every area of his life, and this we must aim for on a world-wide scale.

The personality of man can be molded in almost any direction, good or bad. And when we have decided what we are reasonably assured is good for man, we should work unceasingly to shape personality in that direction.

Almost fifty years ago John B. Watson, a psychologist at Johns

Hopkins University, showed just how a child learns to fear a certain object. This case of Albert and the white rat may be found in almost any introductory psychology text book. Watson found out that Albert at first was not afraid of a white rat. Really the boy was just curious and wanted to touch the rat. But when he reached out to touch the rat, a loud unpleasant noise was sounded behind the child. The noise frightened him. The frightening noise became closely associated with the rat as it was repeated, and finally, through this process of the constant association of the unpleasant noise with the animal, Albert came to fear the rat.[2]

Later Dr. Mary C. Jones at Columbia University showed that in about the same way you could take a child who had already learned to be afraid of an object and teach him not to fear it.[3] This was a little boy named Peter who was afraid of a pet rabbit. By the process of repeatedly associating pleasant things with the rabbit, Peter learned not to be afraid of it.

Although people are born different, their personalities can to a great degree be shaped by the learning process. And everything in the environment teaches something. People are usually the most important part of the environment and have the greatest influence in shaping personality.

All living organisms with some intelligence can be changed through learning experiences. A psychologist by the name of Kuo raised kittens and mice in the same cages and later the cat would never attack his cagemate. Even when the mature cat was very hungry it would still not attack the mouse.[4]

What if greed, anger, jealousy, and crippling fear were all greatly reduced? These are all learned. We can prevent them to a great extent. We can teach good-will toward men. Yes, this is an ideal picture! But the point is that we can come closer and closer to this ideal with a great deal of planning and a great deal of hard work. What could people become in an atmosphere like that? It would be hard to predict.

Dr. Gene L. Schwilck at Union College was responsible for an excellent study showing the relationship of school learning to a moral code.[5] He divided seventy-four boys into two groups that were generally equal. These boys were distributed from grade five through grade eight.

Group I was the object of direct character education, particularly the principle of giving the welfare of the group a higher priority than one's own individual welfare. You will remember that Alfred Adler had emphasized this principle in his "social interest" as being the real hope for humanity in the future. The opposite of it is ego-centricity which is essentially the worst kind of selfishness, and is responsible for man's unhappiness and most of the trouble he has.

Group II which might be called a control group spent the same amount of time in constructive study as Group I, but Group II studied largely vocational problems without the ethical principle.

Numerous tests with both groups, many of them of a practical nature, showed that Group I had learned the ethical principle well and would apply it to everyday problems. Group II had experienced no such change.

Ethical principles that make for better living can definitely be learned. They can be learned after early childhood has passed and they can be well learned and practiced in daily living. They can be taught in the schools, but most of us agree that homes, churches, and schools should unite in teaching ways of life that are better for all of us.

Improvement in the environment can bring about some very amazing changes. One of the clearest ways to see this is in the I.Q. score. Dr. Paul H. Mussen, child psychologist at the University of California, gives the account of a boy whose I.Q. improved by 50 points.[6] When it was first measured the boy's father had tuberculosis and the mother had to go to work. During this period of trouble the boy was "restless, sensitive, and shy," and sick a great deal. His I.Q. measured 113.

When the father became well, the boy's school adjustment was much improved. He was reported to have unusual ability to concentrate and when next tested, his I.Q. had risen to 163!

What Can Man Become?

My own feeling is that man can develop far beyond anything we now know. I believe this is true about his intelligence, his achievement, his creativity, his capacity to love and be loved, and his capacity for joy.

If children were placed in ideal surroundings, with an abundance of affection, where innate curiosity would be nurtured rather than stifled, where the positive emotions held sway, and where learning and well-rounded development were magnified, what would be the limits of their growth? Howard Fast has treated this problem imaginatively in a superb short story entitled *The First Men*, in which a team of sympathetic adults received a large government grant to experiment with rearing children in the most favorable environment possible, as understood by behavioral scientists.[7] A large tract of land was purchased for the location of the experiment.

The major provisions for these children of high potential were an atmosphere of abundant love and understanding, and an opportunity to learn. As the leader of the experiment said, "We are simply taking a group of very gifted children and giving them knowledge and love."

In an atmosphere free from jealousy, fear, hatred, and all the negative forces of a humanity "self-deluded and superstitious and sick and irrational and clinging to legends and phantasies and ghosts," the children grew up healthy, happy, and loving. They learned rapidly from their friendly, learned teachers. At a very early age they began to surpass their teachers.

A world-renowned physicist taught the children as much as he knew. Then the children began teaching him. They advanced so far beyond him that he could not understand their concepts or the symbols by which their concepts were represented.

Such was the affection and understanding which grew up between the children themselves that they worked and thought and created together in complete harmony. One of the anthropologists expressed this in his comment, "Mankind will begin, here in this place, to fulfill a part of its intended destiny—to become a single, wonderful unit, a whole—almost in the words of your poet, John Donne, who sensed what we have all sensed at one time, that no man is an island." The project leader had reported, "In effect, we are teaching a single mind, a mind composed of the unblocked, unfettered talent of forty superb children."

The project leader later summed it up in the last paragraph of a letter, "Man will change, and he will become what he was intended to be, and he will reach out with love and knowledge to all the universes of the firmament. Isn't this what man has always dreamt of, no war, or hatred, or hunger or sickness or death . . . ?"

While this story is fiction, perhaps it is also a glimpse into the future, and as such it may be very true. Such glimpses into the future serve to give us faith and energy now to work toward these beckoning goals for the human race.

With what we know now and the tools we possess for social betterment, we can radically improve man and his society. We can create for ourselves and our children a new and improved nation. With great effort and cooperation we might also create a new world —and this is what we must and will do, for we are now entering the era in which we know it is possible and can see the ways to do it.

This, then, is the world of promise, the world of the future existing now in the minds of many people. It is an ideal world that can become the actual world if we will make it so. It is our enduring confidence that man will make it so.

The late Bertrand Russell, speaking before the UNESCO General Conference gave it beautiful expression as he said:

> I see before me a shining vision: a world where none are hungry; where few are ill; where work is pleasant and not excessive; where kindly feeling is common and where men released from fear create delight for eye and ear and heart. Beyond all reason, I am unconquerably persuaded that this will come.[8]

FOOTNOTES

1. W. F. Dove, "A study of individuality in nutrition in stenets; of the causes and effects of variation in the selection of food," *American Naturalist* 69 (1935), 469–544.

2. John B. Watson and Rosalie Raynor, "Conditioned emotional reaction," *Journal of Experimental Psychology* 3 (1920), 1–14. See also Robert I. Watson, *The Great Psychologists* (New York, J. B. Lippincott Co., 1963), pp. 398–99.

3. Mary C. Jones, "A Laboratory Study of Fear: The Case of Peter," *The Pedagogical Seminary* 31 (1924), 308–15.

4. Zing Yong Kuo, "The Genesis of the Cat's Response to the Rat," *Journal of Comparative Psychology* 22 (1930), 30–35; idem, "Further Study on the Behavior of the Cat Toward the Rat," *Journal of Comparative Psychology* 25 (1933), 1–8.

5. Gene L. Schwilck, "An experimental study of the effectiveness of direct and indirect methods of character education," *Union College Studies of Character Research*, vol. 1, no. 14, pp. 201–229.

6. Paul H. Mussen, *The Psychological Development of the Child* (Englewood Cliffs, N.J.: Prentice-Hall, 1963), p. 51.

7. Howard Fast, "The First Men," in *The Edge of Tomorrow* (New York: Bantam Books, 1961), pp. 14–30.

8. UNESCO, *Records of The General Conference—8th Session—1954* (New York: UNESCO Publications Center), p. 134.